How to Fail as an Author

an Author

Forty Years of Trying to Become Rich and Famous

Steven E. Wedel

MoonHowler Press

MoonHowler Press

Book Cover by Steven E. Wedel

Illustrations by Canva

First edition 2024

CONTENTS

FOREWORD

There are a lot of things one ought to know about Steve Wedel, some of which won't incriminate you by association, but more on that later, I promise. The first thing I came to know about Steve was a bit over twenty years ago when I was writing for the now defunct indie magazine, *Insidious Reflections*. Somewhere along the line, editor Chris Hedges mentioned this werewolf guy named Wedel. I believe the magazine ran an interview or two of Steve and that I may have even interviewed him myself around that time, but I'm almost as old as Steve is now and long-term memories can be a funny thing.

One thing my memory won't let me forget is that the first book or three of Steve's I read back then (don't ask which ones I started with – my memory, remember?) made me realize this Steve fella could *write*. And not just write, but write with the kind of intricate power that belied his relative obscurity of fame. Sometime after *Insidious Reflections* ran its course, I began writing for a website called Fear Zone (also long gone). The editor-in-chief for that one was a friend of Steve's and a friend of mine named Gregory Lamberson. Greg arranged to have me conduct an in-depth interview with Steve and, as part of my homework/research, Greg mailed me some of his personal copies of Steve's books. I believe the titles included a collection of wolfish tales called *Call to the Hunt*, as well as a couple of novellas. Not only did I discover how Steve all but reinvented the werewolf mythos with humanizing, relatable characters, but he could also write the hell out of a terrifying ghost story with *Seven Days in Benevolence* while also bringing me to tears with his haunting tale of age and distorted memories with *Little Graveyard on the Prairie*. I would go on to write a lengthy article for Fear Zone based on all of Steve's Werewolf Saga books to date at that point. There was no turning back for me then. I would go on to read damn near everything he published, some before he published them, most of which I have signed.

During the process of reading Steve, of interviewing him a handful more times and reviewing his work, somewhere along the line we became friends. I would even get the joy of reading books well before they were formatted for publication. And, although I wasn't much of a romance fan, I applauded Steve for writing in this genre under a unique pen name, which you'll learn about in this book. I also applauded Steve for somehow linking up with *New York Times* best-selling author Carrie Jones for a pair of young adult novels, one of which I read and enjoyed immensely. And before you ask, no, our friendship was not based on him showing me how to turn into a werewolf, which is just as well since I have cats and their fur alone is enough to clean up on the regular without me adding to it. As crazy as it sounds, fans of Steve's have indeed asked him how to become a werewolf, so maybe they know something I don't, which is okay because I know something they don't.

I know that Steve's fame and fortune co-exist in obscene opposition of his talent, a hill I won't hesitate to stick a flag in and defend until my last breath. Maybe he just needs a good agent. He'll tell you in this book why that hasn't happened yet. Or maybe a reputable marketing manager with a proven track record is all he's missing to become a household name. He tells us in this book why that is tricky, too. Hell, maybe he just needs to put himself out there, go to all the conventions, meet all the writers and readers in person and get better recognized among his peers and potential target readers so that he can earn their reverence and collective support. Oh yea, you better believe he'll be telling you why that, too, hasn't been quite as easy as it sounds.

I know that most readers of (insert genre here) don't know who Steve Wedel is. I hope this book changes that a bit, and not just because his name is obviously written on the book as its author. I know that to read Steve for the first time is to wonder where the hell he's been hiding out your whole reading life. At least that's how it went for me. If it goes the same for you, then I envy you the fresh thrill of catching up with his impressive body of work up to here, which leads me to my next point.

I'm confident in saying that given the chance, you'll never regret giving his work a try. Go ahead, start anywhere. Just start. Like werewolves? I'll repeat, Steve damn near reinvented them. He made them not only humanly relatable, but also terrifyingly feral in the most brutal way you would want to imagine them. Nightmare fuel, heartache, high stakes plot twists and intensity galore all run rampant throughout his continuing *Werewolf Saga*. Like a good old-fashioned spooky ghost story? His novella, *Seven Days In Benevolence*, stands as one of the most unsettling haunted house stories I've read to date. If you prefer your ghosts to be a bit more human, then *Little Graveyard On the Prairie* has you covered like a second skin. Like your monsters living next door? *A Light Beyond* hammers home the true meaning of fatal attraction in a way that's as shocking as it is resonating and profoundly sad. What's that? You prefer monsters that could never exist in our world except as a worst case fantastic scenario? *Mother* will fit the bill like a bottomless pit of despair while leaving you reeling from the impossible atrocities within while wanting to call up the author to either make sure he is alright, or so he can assure you that everything's going to be alright for you. *Amara's Prayer* offers a similar traumatizing affect, but if you prefer your story-telling a bit more personal and truer to life, *The Lost Pages Bookstore* will suck you in until you don't want back out again until you've learned all there is to learn from the complex, flawed lives you uncover inside. Oh, you're a younger reader who isn't quite ready to leap into the more intense stuff? No FOMO for you because *Love Curse* or *After Obsession* will not only solidify a nearly addiction to reading, it will also remind you you're not alone with the painful tribulations of growing up. Rest assured you can find a friend in Steve's books, and an enemy or two who will be just as captivating.

For those who reckon they need a book that's apt to make you feel as though you'll need to shake the dust off your cowboy hat and jangle your spurs for good effect ...Yeah, Steve has you covered there with some outstanding westerns within his Jacob Wolf series. You can even read Steve to your kids without warping them with his children's book, *Shim and Shay's Wish*. For the hopeless and hopeful romantics alike? A whole world of heartache and steamy intrigue awaits you if only you do a search of Steve's alter ego, Adri Amanti. And let's face it, sometimes what we need the most is to escape the entirety of our world and try out another built on fantastical proportions of pure imagination and masterful world-building. By now you might be expecting Steve to have you covered there, too. Well, you'd be right thanks to his epic series, *The Saga of Tarod the Nine-Fingered*.

At this point, I would be remiss to not point out the one book, that one seemingly innocuous book, which brought Steve's professional teaching career to its knees before kicking it face-down into the gutter. The book which should never have been so consequential to Steve's well being is *The Teacher*. I won't spoil Steve's thunder by giving up all the beans here, but believe me when I say that this book swung an undeserved swing of the shovel to his face in ways no book should ever have the room to do to any writer. Yet, Steve took the hit — what choice did he have, really? — and has used the injustice of it all to buckle down doing what he does best outside of teaching, which is telling stories only he can tell. Only now, perhaps he is writing them with more tenacity, as though he is writing for his life, which, in many ways, he is. The stakes would certainly support this theory.

Alright, one last thing I know about Steve that's worth mentioning before I get out of your way so you can enjoy and learn from the rest of this book, which is, of course, the reason you opened it in the first place. Throughout the twenty or so years I've known Steve as an author and, eventually, as a friend, there's one thing which has always rung loud and clear and consistent, and that's that he may be the humblest, most modest to the point of self-deprecating writer I know. The title to this book? Go ahead and pour some salt on that. I mean, the man's not wrong; he does indeed know several ways to fail as a writer, as he graciously demonstrates in the book you now hold in your hands. As I think we can all understand, there are often just as much, if not more lessons to be learned from screwing up as there are in getting it right. What's that thing Thomas Edison once said after figuring out how to make his light bulb light up? Something about how he didn't fail a gazillion times before finally getting it right, he just figured out a gazillion ways it couldn't work so he could find the one way it would. Maybe that's true for Steve. Or maybe not. Make no mistake, however, that the one thing Steve has never appeared to have gotten wrong is the one thing he seems simply built to do. That thing? It's to keep writing the type of stories that make any reader question why this guy isn't mentioned among the best-selling novelists of our generation. I have no doubt that for Steve, writing stories is much more than a choice. For writers like Steve, it's the only way. Surely, it's up to his hard-earned success to catch up to his talent, his dogged determination as a writer, and not the other way around. Of that I am convinced, despite all the odds that Steve shamelessly reflects on in each of the chapters before you.

Sure, this *is* a book about how to fail as a writer, but it's also about how to persevere as one, too. Considering Steve's story is hardly over, I've no doubt that all this failing business he's been doing over the years, while hardly paved in gold, will eventually lead to a place of success built upon the legacy of a man who was born to write and writes damn well. Maybe then, the rest of the world will know who Steve Wedel is and can join me on that hill to howl his praise across the void until it howls back.

By now, I hope you're starting to get a better sense of who this moon howler named Steve Wedel is because, make no mistake: He wants you to learn from his mistakes. He wants you to take his fumbles, his soured experiences, his every misstep, and use them to elevate your own experience in this writing thing of ours. He wants you to heed his cautions so that you never have to consider writing your own book about how to fail as an author because he did all the failing for you. That's who Steve Wedel is.

If you happen to be reading this from the vantage point of a reader who may not be planning to write your own stories, I imagine you won't be able to view the authors you enjoy reading through the same lens. I'm sure you never thought writing and publishing stories wasn't exactly easy, but now you know just how soul crushing of an endeavor it is and what it takes for those who are born to write to keep grinding those stories out, not just because they want to, but because they must. I would implore you, with your newfound perspective, to consider leaving a review whenever you read a book you enjoy, knowing that every little bit helps the writer, helps them get a bit more traction, helps them know that all their effort and struggles doing the thing they love to do is being appreciated. It matters.

And you never know, maybe that one kind review you leave on Amazon may just be the thing writers like Steve need on those days when they may wonder what the hell they're doing with their life. Your short review or social media post mentioning their work or sharing their latest book's image and/or order link may be the life preserver they need to write another day.

As for Steve's writing life, he's managed to craft his own life preserver stitched together by the leftover pieces of lessons learned the hard way. Some of those pieces are most certainly threadbare by now and hardly holding it together after years of neglect since moving on from whence they came, but they'll still encompass the overall effect of keeping you afloat where Steve has previously sunk. Whether your goal is to land an agent who will propel your career forward, or you're considering the best home for your creative baby, or banging your head against the wall of marketing, or wondering how your writing ambitions may or may not sabotage your day job, just remember that it could always be worse. You could be drowning in self-doubt without this proverbial life preserver cast out to you with best intentions and aspirations even as its giver continues to fight to the top of the surface so that you may be assisted by the pull of his wake.

It's up to you how far you allow this stitched together writer's life preserver to take your creative talent, but as for Steve? Well, let me put it this way: if there's an island where only the most talented, beaten down, hardworking writers gather once they've hit their mark, then you can bet the house Steve will be waiting there for you to join him in basking in the glow of how to fail – and win – as a writer, sharks be damned.

INTRODUCTION

W riting is hard work. Whether you're writing a memoir using real people and places or crafting an epic fantasy set in a world completely different than ours — or science fiction in an alternate universe — you have to keep track of characters' eye and hair colors, their height, weight, mannerisms, speech quirks, etc., plus settings, conflicts, themes, and all those other literary elements.

Then there's the editing. The proofreading. The polishing and convincing yourself that you really are a good enough author to put your work out there for other people to see.

That's when it really gets hard. Do you look for a traditional book deal with one of the major publishers? You'll need a literary agent for that. Do you go with an established independent or genre publisher with a stable of successful authors and a track record of success? What about that new little publisher looking for manuscripts and bubbling with enthusiasm? Or do you go the indie route and self publish? Exclusive with Amazon, or wide distribution?

Once those decisions are made and your book is published, then you have to worry about marketing. You went with the traditional publisher and think you don't have to market? Think again! No matter how your baby is birthed into the world, until you're a bestseller, you are the chief marketing officer for your book.

Oh, and don't forget that you need to be writing your next book, too.

Writing is a business. It's a job. To be successful, you have to treat it that way. It's a great job. No doubt about that. It's a job with a lot of freedom, but it's also a job where you'll only get out of it what you put into it.

I'm here to help you get more out of it by avoiding the legion of mistakes I've made over the course of my career.

Who am I?

I'm going to assume you know my name. If not, go back and peep the cover of the book. As of the writing of this book, I have been submitting creative written works in hopes of publication for almost 40 years. Yes, I'm old. I submitted a draft of eight commandments once and Moses replied with a form letter rejection.

In those 40 years, I've made nearly every mistake an author can make. I've also published around 40 short stories, some poems, hundreds of newspaper and magazine articles, and as of now, about 50 novels under my name and a couple of pseudonyms. I've won awards for fiction and non-fiction ... and maybe poetry; we'll talk about that later. I've worked with tiny start-up publishers, major publishers, had literary agents, and have self-published.

The only mistake I know of that I haven't made is outright paying for publication through a vanity press.

Despite all of this ... despite the hundreds of thousands or perhaps millions of words I've had published over the past four decades, I'm not making a living off my writing. Not yet. Did I mention that writing is hard work?

So, a little more about me. I learned I enjoyed writing when I was in high school in the early 1980s. Yes, back in the days you could catch a buzz from the Aquanet fumes coming off the big hair in the school hallways. I took what was supposed to be a "blow-off" Creative Writing class and instead met the woman who would introduce me to writing as something more than the way to complete an assignment. But it was a few years after that when I began to actually submit my writing for publication.

For most of my career I've been known as a horror author and most readers who have heard of me at all will associate me with my books about werewolves. I'm cool with that, at least until they ask me how they can become werewolves, too. (No, seriously, it happens.) I've dabbled in a lot of other genres, including children's books, young adult paranormals, thrillers, romance, erotica, sword-and-sorcery fantasy, westerns, and literary fiction. This is my second non-fiction book.

I really have just about done it all. And most of it went unnoticed.

Why Does This Book Exist?

Over the past few years, I've become much more serious about making a living from my writing. To that end, I've read a lot of books on publishing, marketing, creating income streams, running a business, etc. Some of the books have been really good. Some have not been all that helpful. Few of them really discussed the failures encountered along the way or, if they did, they were in areas outside the realm of what I've experienced.

Maybe that author started with money and learned how to use Amazon ads by losing a lot of money. As a poor author living on a teacher's salary, that's never been the case with me. I can learn from that author's mistakes, but until I have money to effectively run ads, that's not a problem.

Wanting to see my name, my stories, my ideas in print so bad that I ignore a lot of red flags is a problem I definitely can relate to, and I know it's one a lot of beginning authors struggle with, even if they won't admit it. How do you recognize the signs that a publisher or an offer might not be all you really need it to be?

After reading those books and thinking back over the ups and downs of my career, I decided to write this book. Hopefully it will warn you about things to avoid as you work to become a household name. But maybe it will only entertain you in a Three Stooges kind of way. If any of the old folks who have been playing the game as long as me read it, they'll smile fondly over memories of times and technology come and gone.

I'll try to be entertaining and still appropriate for all audiences.

How Will It Help You?

My goal is to help you write better, publish better, market better, and earn more money from your work. But I also want you to come away knowing that if you're writing just for pleasure and you're happy with one or two book sales per year, that is perfectly okay. I hope you will still find some nuggets you can use.

Mostly, though, I want to give you hope and the courage to persevere in the face of form letter rejections, silence from those you query, massive editorial changes, poor sales, poor reviews, and the depression that comes with being a creative person in a capitalist society. It can be a rough ride, but I know you can do it.

Are you ready to be entertained by my comedy of errors and maybe learn from what hindsight has taught me?

THE BUILDING BLOCKS

I have always loved to read. My mom, who never progressed past eighth grade, gave me that gift from the very beginning with books like *The Teddy Bear Twins* and *A Pickle for a Nickel*, which we read over and over when I was very young. We were regulars at the Public Library of Enid and Garfield County in northern Oklahoma, and later, she would jump through a lot of hoops to buy me birthday and Christmas gifts of books in a city without a bookstore decades before Amazon.com became a thing.

I've spent almost twenty years as an English teacher, mostly at the high school level. Before that, I did 10 years as a newspaper reporter or corporate writer or public relations hack.

Words and language and stories have always been important to me.

Good grades in school weren't that kind of priority, though. School was just something I had to do because my parents made me go. I didn't like it. I wasn't popular. The teachers were usually boring. We were inside most of the day. And, later, there were bullies. I passed because I had to, and it was shameful to fail a class. This included my

English classes. I did enough to get by with a C, or maybe a B, and that was good enough.

Things were different in the early 1980s. In Enid, Oklahoma, at least, you didn't go to high school until 10th grade, at which point you had to take Composition I and II. Kids who did well were invited to take Composition III. I was not invited. There were literature classes. American Literature was required. I took more because, you know, I had to be there, had to take classes, so I took classes where I could read; Short Fiction and Non-Fiction with Mrs. Falls and The Novel with Mrs. Walker were my favorites.

Today, kids enter high school in the ninth grade and take English I. As sophomores they take English II (World Literature), and as juniors they take English III (American Literature), finishing as seniors with English IV (British Literature). Despite having parenthetical names involving literature, this is also where students do the bulk of their academic writing.

At Longfellow Junior High School, I remember having a couple of old battle axes for English teachers. Mrs. LaCroix was the eighth grade teacher who made us memorize and recite every preposition. I'm not good at memorizing and it took me forever to get all of them. Mrs. Roberson in ninth grade was probably the scariest and strictest teacher I ever had. There was no forgiveness in that woman. We had to do note card book reviews and she had a page requirement for the grade. Anything we read and reviewed after that was one point extra credit for every page we read. The first card had to be done in pencil. She would edit it, then we had to redo it in pen. I read *Ivanhoe* for 700 points of extra credit, but because I was a day late with my inked card I lost those points. Junior high was brutal in so many ways.

My high school teachers were, to use today's slang, more chill. I learned from them, but they let me slide by with some stuff that would come back to haunt me later. Here are a couple of anecdotes about my high school writing.

In Composition I, Mrs. Dragoon made us write a short story. I was just turned on to horror movies at that time thanks to seeing *Halloween II* at the downtown theater. So I wrote my first-ever horror story about a teenage boy who was bullied and humiliated at a party, which led to him going on a gleefully and graphically described murderous rampage of revenge. Mrs. Dragoon was shocked that such a quiet boy would write such a violent story. She gave me an A on the assignment. She liked horror and rock music and really wasn't "The Dragon Lady" that people called her.

Sadly, my story "Insanity" has been lost and the world is deprived of that masterpiece. I'm sure if I had it and looked at it today, the biggest horror would be the grammatical and punctuation errors throughout it.

My junior year, I met Mrs. Walker when I took her Creative Writing class. Wilda Walker was a poet, and she loved teaching poetry. She did make us write a short story, and I produced some drivel about a guy going to prison and his girlfriend not waiting for him and he was all sad. I don't remember the details or the title, but I remember even I knew it wasn't very good, but was still hurt that I only got a B on it.

My first writing accolades came because of Mrs. Walker. She held an annual poetry contest open to any student in the school. She bought the prizes herself. That year, I took second place with my poem about a shipwreck survivor in a lifeboat who was thrilled to find land only to be killed when the boat hit some rocks. You see, I've never been a fan of happy endings. Later, Mrs. Walker announced that I and a girl I can't remember were the best poets she had that year.

I thought I was pretty hot stuff, at least in writing.

I was a fool.

That Ain't Good Grammar

Once upon a time, in about 1983, as a senior in high school, I sat at the desk in my bedroom one evening and wrote a story by hand in a notebook. It must not have been too bad — not like "Insanity" — because I showed it to my mom.

"Why did you write that?" she asked.

"Because I wanted to."

"It's not an assignment for school?" she asked.

"No."

My mom loved books, but I guess she'd never considered the possibility that I'd want to write stories on my own. I had the bug, though, and it was quickly burrowing deep into my psyche. Mom and Dad bought me my first typewriter for my high school graduation in 1984. A year later, I got married, and shortly after that I began submitting poetry and stories for publication.

I'll talk more about some of this stuff later, but at the time the hot magazines for horror short stories were *Twilight Zone* and *Night Cry*, with *The Magazine of Fantasy and Science Fiction* taking some crossover stories. I often worked overnight sweeping and mopping the floors of a grocery story. When I finished early, I'd take one of those magazines off the rack and find a quiet place away from the older guys stocking shelves and read until the manager showed up to open the store. I dreamed about having my own stories in those magazines.

Stephen King ruled the roost and everything he did to become the king was studied, so there were the men's magazines to consider submitting work to ... not that my girlfriend/wife would let me actually buy them; there were limits to my allowable research. And then there were the 1980s' equivalent of the 1930s' pulps, most notably David

B. Silva's *The Horror Show*. After that, were other good magazines that didn't pay authors, and then there were the digests made on the new-fangled photocopier machines, which also didn't pay and barely had distribution outside the publisher's and authors' circle of friends.

Depending on my financial situation at the start of the year, or my mom's willingness to supply it for Christmas, I'd use my own copy of the year's *Writer's Market* or go to the library to borrow theirs. I'd start with the top-paying markets, then work my way down to the photocopied 'zines, sending my stories out in hopes somebody would publish them.

Me with my Writer's Market and my dog Bilbo in about 1990 or so.

For years this went on. Money was tight and it was an expense we couldn't really afford, but I talked my wife into letting me subscribe to a few of the magazines in hopes that would give me an edge over other writers who couldn't show they were regular readers. It didn't help.

I learned what the dreaded "form-letter rejection" was. "Dear Author, thank you for your recent submission to Boogity-Oogity magazine. Your writing shows great promise but our editors decided this story is not right for us at this time." It was maddening! What was wrong with the story? How can I make it right for you?

No matter how heartbreaking they were, I kept every one of those rejection letters. But unfortunately, about 30 years after they started coming in, I got divorced and those files were destroyed. I'm not telling you that just to be bitter or cast shade, but to explain why I can no longer tell you the name of the editor who finally took a few minutes to write an actual letter telling me some of what I was doing wrong.

"You need to work on your grammar. For instance, you often use 'seen' where you should say 'saw'."

How humiliating is that?

I knew why I made that particular error, and if you don't laugh at anything else in this book, I feel pretty certain you'll laugh at the ridiculousness of this. I've lived in Oklahoma all my life and my voice has that kind of twang that only sounds right in country music. In my mind, writing something like, "Jimmy saw the monster rise like smoke from beneath his bed" sounded just as hick as, "I done saw that spotted dog swimmin' in the crick out yonder." So, I used "seen" instead because I felt like it sounded more sophisticated.

My junior high teachers should have hunted me down and put me out of everyone's misery.

Since they didn't, and I really, really, really wanted to be a rich and famous author, I figured I had to fix my grammar instead.

But how? I was several years removed from high school and college wasn't an option for various reasons. There was no YouTube. No Khan Academy. No internet, ya know.

Fortunately, my little city on the prairie had a mall that, back then, was still pretty new and wasn't a nearly empty shell like it is today. So, off I went to either B. Dalton's or Waldenbooks in search of a grammar book. Good Lord, I was going to spend money on a textbook. What was the world coming to?

I returned home with a red paperback copy of *A New Guide to Better Writing* by Rudolf Ficsch, Ph.D., and A.H. Lass. A circle graphic on the cover promised it would be "Lively, Authoritative, Effective." Professor Roscoe Ellard of Columbia University's School of Journalism promised in his blurb that I had just secured, "The famous book that can teach anyone to write fluently and well ... Fresh and practical."

A New Guide to Better Writing is what I used to teach myself grammar after refusing to pay much attention in school.

Well, most of the promises on the cover were true, but I can assure you that, like every other grammar textbook I've seen in my 58 years, it was not "lively." Opening the book to write this book of my own, I found that I still have a bookmark between pages 206 and 207, where I finally learned about past participial verb tenses and the difference between see, saw, and seen. You better believe that I was an absolute grammar Nazi about those during my teaching career.

It isn't enough to have a creative spark or vivid imagination, or even to understand things like beginning, middle, end, rising action, falling action, denouement, setting, etc. To make it as an author, you absolutely must know the very basics of the language. What if an editor tells you that you have too many adverbs? I can tell you most of my Advanced Placement senior English students came to me unable to circle an adverb in a sentence.

My experiences with rejection letters, each one a testament to my shortcomings as a writer, served as a wake-up call after I was already a few years into what I hoped would be my career. I needed the technical skills to communicate my ideas with precision and clarity. I didn't have it because I'd been lazy in school.

So, the first lesson in my book about writing: never underestimate the power of a strong foundation in the basics of language. Embrace the study of grammar and sentence structure not as a chore, but as a pathway to unlocking your full potential as a wordsmith. Whether you dream of penning bestselling novels or captivating essays or dazzling news stories, remember that every great literary masterpiece is built upon the sturdy framework of sound linguistic principles. As you embark on your own writing journey, let this lesson be your guiding light, illuminating the path to success one grammatically correct sentence at a time.

Seriously, with the tools available today, there are no good reasons for poor grammar. Most word processing programs will fix the mistakes for you if you left-click the words with colorful squiggly lines under them. Plus, there are other programs designed specifically to find and fix mistakes, and you can often use them for free.

Grammar, punctuation, spelling, and all those other things your English teachers bore you with really matter. If you didn't learn them in school, learn them now.

POETIC BEGINNINGS

My writing career began when I was in fourth grade, I guess. I wrote a non-fiction book about dinosaurs, pulling information from a set of encyclopedias and a few kid books I had on the subject. For illustrations, I traced pictures from the other books. Then I stapled the pages together and showed off my book to much acclaim. Kind of.

Two years later, I wrote a short story set in colonial America for a contest about American history. Only three students in my class attempted an entry, and the teacher didn't select mine for the class submission. Apparently, I was supposed to write an essay, not an adventure story about a boy living in the woods during the French and Indian War.

Then came the story "Insanity" in tenth grade, which I mentioned in the previous chapter. I still wasn't thinking of myself as a writer. I just wrote stuff sometimes. Enter Wilda Walker, the high school creative writing teacher mentioned in the last chapter.

Mrs. Walker was a poet. She loved prose, too, but in her heart, poetry reigned supreme. We spent a lot of time in that Creative Writing class focused on writing poetry.

Now, if you know anything about writing careers, you know that writing poetry for a living is the literary equivalent of begging for pennies on a street corner. There's no money in it. However, I think it's the best place for a writer to start.

Writing poetry teaches the poet, or author, the value and economy of words. In most rhymed forms of poetry, the poet must find words that fit within the prescribed framework and, hopefully, have the emphasis on the correct syllables. Poets have to find, test, and use just the right word to convey the particular nuance they mean.

Aromatic has too many syllables.

Smelly doesn't have the right connotation.

Perfumed makes one think of the thing being sprayed with a bottle of manufactured scent.

Nobody knows what redolent means anymore.

Fragrant ... what rhymes with "fragrant" and fits the next line about wet grass?

Punctuation matters in poetry. Should this line end in a period? A semi-colon? No punctuation? How avant-garde would I be to just include any punctuation? I don't know all the rules for it, anyway.

Poetry typically is the shortest form of creative writing, but getting it to come out just right can be difficult, painstaking work that takes hours per line.

Or, you might rip off the perfect poem on the first draft.

I wrote a lot of poetry between 1982 and about 1996. I had a girlfriend who became my wife, so there was a fair amount of really bad love poems. Most, though, took one of two other forms. They were either bleak, depressing, and ended in death, or they were pornographic.

The first of the latter type was written as a junior in high school and was called "Nymphomaniac." Like a lot of my poetry, it was meant to be heavy metal song lyrics. Think of Blackie Lawless of WASP singing,

Nymph-o-maniac

She loves to be

On her back!

I could picture it back in the day.

After high school, at my first full-time job working as a machinist, I would write more such gems on the back of job cards to amuse my co-workers. Sadly, most of those treasures have been lost, with only a few random lines lingering in my memory.

Mrs. Walker never knew about my porno poetry. She did, however, encourage my other poems, which she called "somber." I took second place in her annual poetry contest, winning a hardcover notebook of lined pages where I wrote the "final" draft of a lot of poems. Yeah, that book is lost now, too.

Over the years, I've written a few poems that I still feel are good. Most were horrible to mediocre, but I was learning the language of poetry, the importance of the right word and how to express a thought in the number of lines and syllables that seemed pleasing to the ear. It was good experience.

The Golden Poet

A year after graduation I somehow learned about a thing called World of Poetry. I was only nineteen and had no idea what the real world was like. I think I saw an ad for World of Poetry in *The Writer* magazine, but it doesn't matter how I heard about them. Editor and publisher John Campbell was having a contest and, recalling how I took second place in Mrs. Walker's contest, I was determined to enter.

There was an entry fee. I was newly married and my wife and I were both only working part-time jobs, but we scraped together whatever the entry fee was per poem and I sent in my three best, including the one that placed in the school contest.

Imagine my shock and joy when, weeks or months later, I was notified that I hadn't won a cash prize, but one of my poems was selected to be in their upcoming anthology *Our Western World's Most Beautiful Poems*.

What's this paragraph of the joyous letter about? If I don't buy a copy of the book, they can't guarantee my inclusion? How much is it? $69.95?!?!

My mom paid for two copies of that giant book filled with bad poetry so that she could have one of her own.

I had not yet got all pretentious and begun using my full first name and middle initial like I do now, so the gem you're about to be exposed to was attributed simply to Steve Wedel. This was my contribution to that first anthology:

Lonely is the Sea

When I look out upon the rolling sea,
Lonliness stretches forth its hand to me.
On the beach the seagulls cry,
As the waves roll and sigh.
The very sight grieving my heart,
Piercing through it like a dart.
Always rolling onto the land,
Pulling away the very sand.
It fills my heart with emptiness,
To look upon the sea's loniness.

How about those uncorrected typos? At this point, I can't tell you if they were mine or the typesetter's, but there they are on page 488 of that 11"x8.5" hardcover anthology, mocking me thirty-nine years after the 1985 publication. Also, in 1985, I had yet to actually see an ocean.

Our Western World's Most Beautiful Poems, which includes my first time in print.

And yes, I said first anthology. You see, after the first one, World of Poetry granted me one of their coveted Golden Poet awards. They knew they had a sucker on the line. I kept submitting poems. I appeared in another of their awful anthologies, and was awarded several more of those sought-after Golden Poet awards. When I finally wised up and stopped submitting to them, they gave me the only slightly less prestigious Silver Poet award for excellent poets who were no longer contributing.

This, my friends, was my first – but by no means my last – experience with publishing scams.

No Wasted Effort

I kept writing poetry. Since the local writer's group met on a weekday evening and I worked the night shift at the machine shop, I couldn't join. The only writers' group I could find with a compatible meeting time was the Don Blanding Poetry Society, which just so happened to include my favorite teacher, Wilda Walker. The group published a few chapbook anthologies that included my poetry while I was involved with them.

My biggest poetic triumph was getting one into the pages of *The Writer* magazine. I figured there was no way they would accept one and pay me for it, so I included it in a letter to the editor about how their magazine was helping me toward my goal of becoming a writer so I wouldn't have to keep punching a time clock and feeling like this:

Life on the Clock

The dreariness of tomorrow

Laps onto the shores of today

As I flee the desolation of yesterday.

I still write a poem every once in a while, when the mood strikes. They're not as bad as "Lonely is the Sea," but it still isn't my best form of writing.

There are a few lessons that can be taken from my experience with poetry. The first is that it's a great way for an author to learn the finer points of using the language to say precisely what he or she wants to say in an evocative way.

It can be a fun way to entertain your friends. Poems are short and punchy and can be written about any topic you and your friends enjoy.

And finally, for anything you love, there will be somebody out there more than willing to set up some shady scam to take advantage of you. With writers, that desire to see our work – our names – in print can easily override our common sense and part us from our hard-earned dollars. I'll tell you more horror stories of this variety later on in this book. The key point to remember here is that money flows TO the writer. If you have to pay, stay away.

I'll close this chapter with a scanned page from *Mausoleum* magazine, a publication I'll talk more about later. This poor excuse for a poem is unworthy of the original artwork that accompanied its initial publication.

18

THE VAMPIRE'S KISS

Kiss me, with lips undead.
Feed me Dark Gifts from your veins.
Kiss me, here in my bed,
Let your blood wash clean my pains.

Kiss me that I may die.
Give to me immortal thirst.
Kiss me, I will not cry,
Let me feel a sweet heart burst.

Kiss me, that I may live.
Give me footfalls light as breath.
Kiss me, 'tis yours to give,
I'll watch Time make love to Death.

Steven E. Wedel

My poem, "The Vampire's Kiss" with artwork by Mausoleum maga-zine's publisher, Crow Ravenscar.

GROUP WORK

M ost of the writers I've known in my life are pretty introverted. There are several exceptions to that, but for the most part we're the kind of people who, as Western author Johnny Quarles once told me, will "Sit in the corner of a party and watch the people, the dog, and the fly buzzing around the room" rather than mix and mingle with all those people who'll ask questions and expect us to talk and stuff.

Ironically, if you go to a writers' conference, you'll find nearly everybody in the bar in the evening. We're a whole lot less introverted when we're among our own kind. And maybe have alcohol in us ...

That need to be social, to find our people who understand what we do and what we go through and how it affects our mental health, our relationships, our income, our jobs, and everything else, is as strong with writers as it is with any other person. That often leads us to seek out writers' groups.

When we think of writers' groups, we might imagine everyone sitting around sipping tea, or meeting in a coffee shop, a restaurant or a bar, being like The Inklings and reading our draft of the books that will be bigger than *The Lord of the Rings* or *The Chronicles of Narnia*. But what we generally get is a whole lot different.

I've been a member of a few local writers' groups, a statewide organization, and one international club. I'm about to relate my experience with each of them and then tell you what I've decided in regards to continuing in or seeking out any new groups. My experience is not yours, and you may — hopefully you *will* — have better experiences than I've had.

Remember, this is a book about failing as an author.

DBPS

As stated in the previous chapter, my first experience with a writer's group was in Enid, Oklahoman, The Don Blanding Poetry Society (DBPS). Make no mistake, I was grateful for this group, even if I wanted to be a horror author and not a poet, because it put me around creative people. I was working as a machinist at the time, and most of my co-workers didn't read anything more than maybe the *Playboy* centerfold's turn-ons.

For some reason, the group met in the Enid branch of the Oklahoma Highway Patrol headquarters, which back then was way, way, way out on the western edge of the city. Being poor but of European decent, I lived on the east side of town. Not that Enid is or was all *that* big, but at the time it was pretty much my world. So, once a month, I made the drive.

The president of the group was an elderly lady named Maxine Austin, author of the poetry collection *Spring of the Spirit*. My former teacher Wilda Walker was a member. The only other member name I can remember is Richard Brown. I was the youngest member, probably by about forty years. No, seriously.

We would have our meetings and read poetry and praise each other. Sometimes there would be some gentle critiquing. There was a lot of general conversation, mostly about people and topics I knew (and cared) nothing about.

The meetings were eventually moved to Maxine's home, and, at the time, it was the most expensive house I had ever been in. It was in an older part of town, was two stories, with lots of stained wood and the feeling that it was owned and cared for by a wealthy older widow. The format of the meetings didn't change, only the setting from the sterile state police outpost to the lavish home where she often had a bowl of water and mimosa flowers for fragrance.

As I said before, we published a few chapbook anthologies of poetry. Or maybe it was just a couple. For what they were, they turned out looking pretty good and I enjoy flipping through them all these years later and reading the words of friends who have passed on.

What I got from this group was support, encouragement, and empathy. They knew I wasn't very good, but they understood what I wanted in life and gave me what advice they could. Mostly, though, they understood the need to create with words, the drive to sit down and put words on paper in an effort to leave a mark in the world. That was something I wasn't getting anywhere else.

Live Poets in and Around Enid, an anthology published by the Don Blanding Poetry Society.

In 1993 I was offered a machinist job in Oklahoma City that paid a lot better, so me, my wife, and my one-year-old son moved about ninety miles south, leaving behind our families, our old jobs, and The Don Blanding Poetry Society.

CORA and Other Local Clubs

After settling into "the City" as most Okies refer to our state's capitol metropolitan area, I saw something in the newspaper about the Central Oklahoma Roundtable of Authors (CORA) having an event at one of the shopping malls. A writer's group? I had to go!

Well, that event was a romance cover model contest where half-naked men posed while women screamed like banshees for the one they liked best. There was so much screaming! From my place on the upper level looking down into the food court, I didn't know who was a writer and who was just a horny old woman, but with so many people and so much noise, I believed CORA was a big deal. So, the next time they met, I was there.

Make no mistake, I met some good people there and I did learn some valuable things about writing. Mostly what I learned, though, was to seek out my own kind. Keep in mind, I was only writing horror stories at this time. I was several meetings into my new group before I found out they had only very recently changed their name from Central Oklahoma Romance Authors in hopes of attracting new members from other genres. But most of the members at that time were still romance authors.

There wasn't a genre of smutty vampire romance novels or "knotting" werewolf stories or loving zombies while they're still warm back in the early 1990s. Romance writers of the time really were not interested in reading, critiquing, or even hearing about my stories of hillbilly corpses reanimated with rage held in bear fat or darkness that sucked the fluid out of bodies or the very earlies drafts of what became *Shara*.

CORA had a large number of published authors. All of them were romance authors. Most of the membership was female. I became the newsletter editor for a while before I left. I wanted the experience, I wanted to be important, and I have a hard time saying no when asked to do something. We'll see that crop up again later in this chapter.

Eventually, I did stop going to CORA meetings. I wasn't getting what I needed from them, I got hurt at work, and eventually started attending college in my late twenties.

There was another writers' group on campus that I joined. This was at the University of Central Oklahoma, which had recently changed its name from Central State University. The name of the group was Central State Writers Institute. I remember one meeting where a Western author talked about mistakes writers of the Old West make, such as the magic holster that reloads six-shooters that were empty when the cowboy holstered them. And I remember Iris, the president, crying when she turned over the presidency before graduation. I think I might have become president after that, but I can't remember. My time at UCO ended badly and I've blocked out a lot of it.

In college, I met another serious writer who was also a journalism student. Years later, she and a co-worker at the Oklahoma Supreme Court, along with another friend or two and me. formed a group called Literary Buffet. We would meet for lunch on occasion and exchange manuscript sections and talk about what we'd read. I was, by far, the most prolific of the group. I don't even know how many of my novels I foisted on Gayleen and Paul, the only other members who remained regulars, during the years we met. Neither of them wrote horror or read it much, but they were faithful and honest critique partners.

Gayleen eventually got re-married and moved to Texas, putting an end to that group. I believe you can hire her to edit your manuscript now, if you're so inclined. She has since earned an MFA and specializes in children's stories.

Both CORA and Literary Buffet were affiliate chapters of the Oklahoma Writers Federation, Inc. This umbrella group puts on an annual conference with a contest and attracts writers from all over the region. Their guest list is often impressive. In the early years of my association, I was blown away that they had Tabitha King as a guest (yes, the Tabitha who took her husband Stephen's story *Carrie* out or the trashcan back in the 1970s). The membership, however, seemed to be mostly old ladies who wanted to publish their memoirs, so for many years I dropped out of OWFI. I went back last year when my friend Vickey Malone Kennedy asked me to judge one of their contests and was impressed by how the group has grown and diversified. It's not just octogenarians writing about the Dust Bowl anymore.

Other than the conference, OWFI doesn't have meetings. I'm a token member of one of the affiliate groups, but seldom get to attend the Rose Rock wRiter meetings.

I've tried several times to establish writers' groups. At first, I tried in-person groups based on speculative fiction, then online groups. I've tried forming groups of published independent and small press authors focused on group promotions. Nothing ever came of any of it.

Like group projects in school, writers' groups only work if everyone participates, and when you're an adult with jobs, spouses, kids, etc., it's hard to be committed to one more thing when you could use that time to write.

Horror Writers Association

The Horror Writers Association was founded by some of the biggest names in the genre during the heyday of horror fiction in the 1980s. I used to salivate over the idea of becoming a member of a group that included the likes of Robert R. McCammon, Dean Koontz, and Joe Lansdale.

There are — or were — two levels of membership to HWA, affiliate and active. Anyone who said they wrote horror fiction, poetry, or screenplays could become an affiliate member for $65 per year (that was in the mid-1990s). To be an active member and get to vote for the Bram Stoker Awards, you had to have a certain number of sales at the minimum professional rates per word (three cents at the time; it was up for five cents when I left the group) or a book contract with an advance of $2,500. I wanted to join as an active member, so put it off for quite a while, but finally joined as an affiliate in hopes of finding help getting to that next level.

Early on, there were probably some things I enjoyed about being an HWA member, but I can't remember now what they might have been. What I found was a message board that erupted into flame wars almost daily, often at the instigation of one bully who, for reasons I never learned, was allowed to ridicule less experienced writers as if he was the Great Value Harlan Ellison.

I become the online newsletter editor at some point. I created my own column in which I interviewed member authors about their web sites. Remember, this was all new back then and authors were just figuring out what a "web presence" meant and what worked and what didn't. Between the newsletter and doing profiles for the Horror World web site, I did get to interview some of the biggest names in the genre. Toward the end of my run in HWA, I also became the publicity person. I resigned that position when they wanted me to promote the *Blood Lite* anthology, a book with what I still say is an absolutely ridiculous cover that looks like something drawn and colored by a kindergärtner.

I achieved that active status in HWA, but by then I was over it all. In a message board discussion about membership renewal or dues increase, or something, I commented that I felt like I wasn't getting anything for my money. The president at the time (I can't remember who he was) told me it wasn't about what I was getting, but what I was giving to the organization and the genre. Dude. It's a writers' group, not a religion. I didn't renew and I've never regretted it.

From what I can tell, the HWA is still a hotbed of favoritism, in-fighting, and political correctness. Maybe you or somebody you know is benefiting from membership, but I never did. Most of the genre friends I made back in the day was through the now-defunct Shocklines message board.

So, what's the verdict on writers' groups? Can they help a writer? Are they a good place to at least make friends who'll understand our tortured souls? Eh. Yes and no.

My experience leads me to believe most groups are made up of members who gravitate to a particular genre and tend to stay there.

Or the members are all new to the craft and just want somebody — anybody — to read their million-page masterpiece and tell them they're brilliant.

Or, there is at least one self-righteous egomaniac who believes nobody else has any relevant experience or valuable information to share.

But none of that negates our need or desire to find people who share our passion for creating the written word, finding agents and publishers, and eventually seeing people we don't know reading something we've written as they wait for a bus or let their dog play at the park.

Most local groups will let you visit a couple of times before asking you to join. I would encourage you to do that, put aside your shyness, and mingle with people and ask them if there are other members working in your genre, are at your level or above, and are nice people. If you find a few people who meet that criteria, you've hit the jackpot.

For the bigger groups, I guess it looks good on a resume, but otherwise I just don't see the point. But that's just me. If you want to try it, go for it. It's always better to have your own experience to draw from.

TALES OF TECH

I began my career with a pencil and paper, which is probably how must writers have begun, at least since the days of the feather quill ended. First drafts were done in pencil, and final drafts in ink.

The Typewriter Era

Pen and ink on lined notebook paper was not going to cut it as a professional. So, my senior year of high school, I took a class called Personal Typing and learned the fundamentals of typing on a behemoth Smith-Corona Selectrix, the kind with the ball with different letters all over it. I almost failed that class because the typewriter didn't have correction tape and we got a zero on any paper in which we erased a hole. I had to retype my final because of a hole ... and I put a hole in the revision, too. I think I was typing about 35 words per minute when that semester ended. It was enough, though. Today, I type a little over 100 words per minute. I can type as fast as I think and carry on a conversation with a befuddled and amazed student while I do it.

My graduation gift from high school was a Brother electronic type-writer. I desperately wanted a typewriter, but also didn't want to cost my parents too much money, so I chose this Brother EP-20 unit and was with my mom when she bought it at K-Mart. It was supposed to be $164, but the cashier struggled to read the price tag (nobody scanned bar codes back then) and rang it up as only $64. I thought I should have gotten the other $100 for keeping my mouth shut, but I never did.

This is what my Brother EP-20 electronic looked like.

I typed some short stories on that Brother typewriter, and I probably even submitted them. The problem, though, was that it printed in a light dot matrix. For you young'uns, that means that each letter was a series of dots in the shape of the letter. It was not at all like the firm, solid typewriter letters that are easy to read on a white page. Later, when computers began to take over the world and affordable printers spit out connected and perforated pages, they used dot matrix ... and publishers would say "no dot matrix submissions" in their guidelines because they were hard to read.

It was a year or so later when I convinced my parents to buy me a real typewriter because the little Brother EP-20 couldn't produce work I could send to editors. I chose a Smith-Corona Electra XT. That bad boy had correction tape, so there'd be no holes rubbed through my paper with those weird typing erasers.

For those of you who have never done serious work on a typewriter, it's a lot different than today's computers. First, there are the margins on your page. The left is easily set and the carriage (the rolly thing that holds the paper) will return there when you hit the Return key.

As you type, the carriage moves and, when it's near the right margin, the machine will ding a bell to warn you. Then you have to make a decision. Squeeze off a few more letters? Hyphenate and return? Return immediately? If you fail to return on time, you'll pound one letter over another at the end of your line and, since it's the end of the line, the machine will back-space to the previous letter and white-out that instead of your mess if you try using the correction tape. So, you have to erase by hand, or wait until you remove the page and crack open the little bottle of White-Out.

Top and bottom margins are an-other issue. Every page has to have your name, the story title, and the page number at the top. There is no For-mat button to push on a typewriter. I solved this issue with a template, a piece of paper where I typed the num-

My Smith-Corona Electra XT typewriter.

ber 1 in the top right corner, then numbered all the way to the bottom of the page. Every time I typed a page on a "final" draft of a manuscript, I rolled that numbered page in behind my blank page so I could line up where my header should be, and so I could stop on the same line on every page. Making the template was no small feat. Have you ever tried typing in the very top or bottom corner of a page on a typewriter? It isn't easy!

So, I have a completed story. Uh-oh. I need more suspense before the final reveal of the monster in the box, so I decide to add a scene where our hero thinks he hears a low growl and some panting coming from the box. You know what that means? Retyping almost the whole story, at least from the point where I want to add the scene. There was no cursor to position and begin adding text.

I wrote two drafts of my first novel, *The Prometheus Syndrome*, like this.

The Smith-Corona PWP3 word processor with a flip-up screen that shows about five lines of text as you type.

Composing on a typewriter was a lot of work. No grammar or spelling checker. No cut-and-paste or formatting options. Writing wasn't for the weak or easily distracted.

The computer age was dawning, but money for us was tighter than a ten-gallon butt in five-gallon jeans. At some point in the late 1980s, my wife and I were in a Montgomery Wards store in one of the Oklahoma City malls. I had talked her into letting me upgrade my typewriter to something that saved the work. Computers were, by today's standards, still primitive and very expensive, so I bought a Smith-Corona PWP3 word processor.

This machine opened up big possibilities and reduced my revision work a whole lot. I could store what I wrote on these hard little three-inch diskettes. The diskettes didn't hold a whole lot of data, and it took between five and seven of them to hold a complete novel, but the very fact I could save my work, then pull up what I'd previously written and edit it was simply revolutionary.

I retyped *The Prometheus Syndrome* on the PWP3, then wrote four more novels on it, including *The Living Dark* (unpublished), *The Saga of Tarod the Nine-Fingered, Volume 1*, *We the People* (unpublished), *Scratch* (unpublished), and the short story "Biological Clock" that would be the seed that grew The Werewolf Saga books. I also wrote the first drafts of my children's books, *Shim and Shay's Wish* and *Songbird*, on that machine. All while working full-time as a machinist. I think that's a pretty impressive output for what couldn't have been more than about five years.

Dawning of the Computer Age

In 1993, we made the move to The Village, a little suburb surrounded by Oklahoma City, and I continued to work as a machinist, but for $2 an hour more than I'd been making in Enid, plus I "got" to work overtime. The world was moving on, and it was time for another upgrade to my writing life.

I went to a mall store called Wizard's and bought my first computer. I can't recall now if it was used as it was, or if the store techs had built it out of used parts. I do remember it had an 8088 processor and a whopping 20 megabyte hard drive with 64k of memory. It had drives for two 5 1/2 inch floppy disks, came with a keyboard and a monochrome monitor in which everything was displayed in Cold War green.

Over the next eight or nine years, I made a lot of upgrades to that unit. I think I upgraded the motherboard twice, swapped out one of the 5 1/2" drives for a 3 1/4", added quite a bit of memory, and added, then upgraded a dial-up modem.

Not the one I had, but a similar desktop computer with an 8088 processor and green monochrome monitor.

But in the beginning, I used it as it was. A friend gave me the disks for a version of Wordstar, a word processing program that is nearly forgotten now, but I read at the time that Anne Rice used it. I had to load each disk into memory in the correct order to be able to use the software. It was a pain. I eventually got a pirated version of WordPerfect. I think it was WordPerfect 5.1. It had a blue background and white text ... which tells me I had already upgraded to a VGA monitor by that time.

In the time before Windows, everything started with the DOS prompt. I don't remember all the commands now, but when you turned on the computer, you got a piece of code at the top of your monitor that, I believe, looked like this <C/:> and you had to tell the computer what you wanted to do. So, if I wanted to back up my work-in-progress to a floppy disk in the B drive, I would type in C>copy b:shara and hit Enter, then wait while the computer worked.

To my horror, a friend told me if you typed /format at that original prompt, the computer would erase the hard drive. I was so scared of losing everything on my new computer that I called my wife and warned her never to type that on the computer. She got pretty mad at me for thinking she might do that, and looking back, it would have been a totally random thing for anybody to type, but the fear was real.

I used that computer, upgrading as I could, for about eight or nine years. I wrote my novels *Bold Bounty* (published under my pseudonym Adri Amanti) and *Shara* on it, which really isn't much at all when compared to the output I had with the PWP3, but it was during those eight years that I left machine shops due to a shoulder injury, went to college and earned a bachelor's degree in journalism, went to work for the state's biggest daily newspaper (which totally sapped my creativity for personal writing), and left journalism to become a corporate writer for Conoco, Inc. Conoco had a year of record profit in 2001, and as a result, every employee got to choose an expensive electronic gift. I chose a new desktop computer and donated my old one to my kids' elementary school (after deleting all my stories from the 20MB hard drive, of course).

From there, I've gone through a series of laptops, using them far beyond their expected lifespan because I'm cheap and generally take care of my equipment. I'm currently using an HP that does things I never would have dreamed about when I began writing. I'm writing this book using Scrivener software because I like the outline and notes features, but I write most of my fiction in Atticus because of the ease of formatting and because it's both an app and web-based, so I can work on the same book on any computer. I used MS Word for years and years until Microsoft made it a paid subscription, then I worked in Google Docs for quite a while, but it's rather limiting. It is free, though, and definitely a great tool for the beginning author.

The Information Superhighway

It was the mid-1990s and this new thing called the Internet came on the scene. Yes, style books at the time capitalized "Internet." It was the World Wide Web. The Information Superhighway. It was the future.

But you couldn't just click the Chrome icon and start searching. Oh no. You had to have a subscription with somebody. America On-line (AOL) was the dominant provider at the time, but also one of the more expensive ones. I went with a company called CompuServe.

Of course, this was after I installed a 24bp modem in my first computer. This was more advanced than what you see in movies like *War Games* and *Weird Science* because I didn't have to actually put the telephone headset into a device to dial up CompuServe. I had an internal modem, which meant opening up the central processing unit and installing it in one of the unused card slots. With the internal modem, you simply plugged the phone line from the wall into the Input hole and ran another cord from the Output of the modem to your old-fashioned land-line telephone.

With that set up, I clicked on the CompuServe icon from my Windows 3.1 screen, and away I went ... like a turtle. In winter. Through thick mud.

Bing ... bong ... hissss ... bing bing bing ... buzzzzzzzz

And I was connected. "Nobody pick up the phone! I'm using the modem!" I'd yell through the house.

I could access the internet through CompuServe, but CompuServe didn't really want me doing that. The company wanted me to use their vast array of online features. The only one I remember now is their chat rooms. Once I did find out how to get on the internet, there wasn't really anything to do there. Social media wasn't a thing. No individuals I knew of had a personal web site.

The internet was kind of like having a massive spell book where no one had figured out the magic to record how to use it.

I left CompuServe after a while and signed on with a local provider called Telepath. This was one of my very first entrepreneurial enterprises. I had a "friend" at the time who was a horrible mooch. Like, the guy would order fast food, eat it, then call the restaurant and say there'd been something wrong with it. No, he couldn't bring it back because he'd thrown it out. He'd usually get free food. Anyway, we were going to start a company building web sites, and share my Telepath subscription. Think of this like sharing your Netflix login in modern times. But then he shared it with another friend, so there were three of us using one dial-up account from three different physical addresses and phone numbers, and none of us could log in if one of the others was using it. Guess who was paying the bill.

During this time, I convinced one person to let me build a web site for him. It was my friend, Western author Johnny Quarles. I built the site — and back then you had to build it completely with HTML code because there was no Wordpress or Wix or anything with pre-formatted templates — but Johnny could never find it online. The URL was something like http://www/telepath.com/sewedel/quarles.html. I never figured out why I could pull it up on my computer and he couldn't find it on his. It was an embarrassment.

Telepath figured out what we were doing and asked me about the three locations dialing in, so I said a friend had gotten my password. I changed the password, changed the name of the company to Word-Press Productions, and that was the end of that friendship. Obviously, with only one client who couldn't find the website he'd paid for, the company never took off.

Today, writing without the use of the internet would be almost unthinkable. The amount of research information found online is mind-boggling. Not to mention the communication ability, social media, marketing, etc.

The internet and e-mail has killed the old self-addressed stamped envelope, the SASE required if you wanted your hard copy manuscript returned from the agent or publisher who was turning you down. Now, instead of waiting months to find your brown envelope returned to your mailbox, you know you'll probably just never hear from the agents or editors who aren't interested in the submissions you e-mailed to them. Yay!

Artificial Intelligence and Beyond

As I write this in May 2024, the big technology issue is artificial intelligence. On Facebook, there are groups defending the use of AI, and groups that are very much against using it in any way, shape, or form.

The problem is that some people are feeding a prompt into an AI generator and the computer is writing an entire novel that the "author" then claims as their own and publishes to compete with novels worked and sweated over by real writers.

Where is AI getting the information to write that book? That's one of the sticking points. Several authors are suing some AI companies because they've learned that their published novels have been used to train the AI bots without the authors' permission. So, the AI-generated story is somehow using stuff humans wrote to stitch together "new" material that other people are claiming as original work and making money from.

The same thing is happening with visual arts. The bots steal bits and pieces — including artist signatures — to create "new" artwork based on the given prompt.

To digress a little, I'll say that as a teacher, I absolutely hate artificial intelligence. Too many lazy students use AI to generate their assignments despite being told how easy it is to spot such work. I hate that students have access to it, but when they use it, it's easy to give them a zero on the assignment. See, AI-generated stuff has correct spelling and grammar and uses a bigger vocabulary than the lazy students possess. It is funny to call a kid up to my desk and ask them the meaning of various multi-syllabic words found in his or her essay and listen to their excuses for why they can't remember the meaning of that word right at the moment.

I have used artificial intelligence. I've used it for research, such as in the book *Sycamore Souls*, which I just recently finished. I asked AI several questions about historical events, then used key phrases to look up and verify the information.

As I write this book, I'm also working on the fourth book in my Western series *The Travels of Jacob Wolf*. I didn't have any clear idea for the plot of the book after Jacob leaves his old mentor, so I gave ChatGPT 3 a prompt and asked it to outline a novel. It gave me an outline and I actually liked most of it. Not all. It suggested the villain of the next book be called "Black-Eyed Bart" and that simply isn't going to happen. I also never stick to outlines, even when I generate them myself, but in this case, I used a tool to suggest some things. AI didn't write the book, and I'll never use AI to write a whole book.

I've also put chapters of this book into ChatGPT 3 along with a prompt such as, "Does this chapter contain interesting and informative anecdotes and provide a lesson that will help new authors?" The bot does give some interesting and valuable feedback.

Obviously, over the past 40 years, I have welcomed and embraced new technology in the form of writing machines and software. I write because I have stories that I want to tell. Often, those stories are some sort of therapy for me. If you look at the themes of my novels, you can tell what kind of personal issue I was dealing with at the time I wrote them. The typewriters, computers, and internet have been amazing tools in helping me to express the thoughts, feelings, and stories I want to share.

I don't see where somebody using artificial intelligence can find any joy in publishing a story he or she didn't birth through his or her own brain. Maybe they'll make some money at it. Probably, they'll make more money than I'm making. But I think it's a misuse of technology.

Show me the robot that'll wash my dishes and dust my house so that I have more time to write. That's the artificial intelligence I want to see.

My point here is that there have been many, many advances in the field of writing and mass producing written works, and that will continue. In some cases, like moving from a typewriter to a computer, there are no ethical dilemmas involved. Using artificial intelligence and whatever comes next and next and next blurs the lines and, ultimately, it will be up to you what you embrace and reject.

SHORT STORIES

I f you remember Chapter 2 of this book, you'll recall that my first serious attempts at a writing career were with poetry. Poems are short. The first draft, at least for me, doesn't demand a lot of time. You're in, you're out, you have a finished piece of work to show off.

It's like when a baby begins to crawl. They're mobile, but not graceful, or even coordinated, really. They can get from place to place, slowly, with dirty knees, and they probably can't reach what they want once they get there.

That makes the short story the toddler stage of a writing career. Toddlers are little walkers. More coordinated and with better reach than a crawling infant, but not at all like an adult.

I can hear you screaming at me about my extended analogy. You know where it's going, and you know some people, maybe only a few, but some people have made a great living off brilliant short stories that are nothing like the clumsy toddler.

Uh-huh. Very, very few, especially since the middle of the Twentieth Century. Novels are where the money is, so if I forget to extend my analogy to the chapter where I talk about writing novels, just know that I meant to dazzle you with that bit of brilliance.

For now, I'm going to talk about how advancing to short stories from poems was like my personal toddler stage of writing.

Short stories take more time than poetry. They require characterization, plot, conflict, rising action, falling action, and all those other things your English teachers hammered into you. But there are no subplots and the cast is limited, so it isn't as complicated as a full novel. In that way, it's toddling. Not running. Certainly not dancing.

Slicks and Pulps

I don't remember the first story I wrote once I set my mind on the idea of becoming a professional author. I remember sitting in the back bedroom of our two-bedroom house on East Chestnut in Enid, banging out several stories, including "Elijah," "The Hitchhiker," "Grandpa Frost," "The House Beside Soldred Quarry," and many others. "The Hitchhiker" was every bit as hackneyed as you're thinking and has been lost without ever being published.

I wrote a lot of ghost stories during that time, too. I was very interested in the value of the human soul, how to attach it to another person, whether it could be split, etc.

When I was sixteen years old, I found a book in an Evans Drug store called *13 Horrors of Halloween*. Halloween having always been my favorite holiday, I bought the thin anthology edited by some guy named Isaac Asimov and absolutely loved it. That sent me to one of the two bookstores in our new Oakwood Mall in search of more. I told the clerk I wanted horror stories, and left with Stephen King's *Night Shift* and an H.P. Lovecraft collection called *Bloodcurdling Tales of Horror and the Macabre*. These two books, and a few stories from the Halloween anthology, were the inspiration for most of my early stories.

So, I wrote short horror stories. I took my typewritten pages with no eraser holes, but with a few handwritten corrections, put them in large brown envelopes, drove to the post office, and explained I needed to mail this and pay for return postage and put this envelope inside. You'd be surprised to know the number of times I, a teenager or in my early twenties, had to explain how to weigh and price a submission and self-addressed stamped envelop to postal clerks who obviously didn't encounter many writer-types.

Invariably, the stories came back. See Chapter One for a good part of why.

But, this chapter is about where I was sending those early stories.

Twilight Zone magazine was my Mount Everest. It was a "slick" magazine, meaning the pages were glossy, high quality, and made to last. They also paid professional rates, which at the time was three cents per word. All the big name speculative fiction authors of the time were publishing in *Twilight Zone*.

On the same level in terms of pay were a couple of "pulp" digest-sized magazines, *Night Cry* and *The Magazine of Fantasy and Science Fiction*. Then there was an Alfred Hitchcock magazine for stories that had more of a mystery flavor than horror, but sometimes a good horror story worked its way in there. It was the 1980s and horror was hot stuff.

I never did better than a form letter rejection from any of these magazines, but they were my first targets for just about everything.

Because Stephen King did it, I also considered and occasionally submitted to men's magazines, aka dirty magazines. *Playboy* was obviously the top of the line at the time, paying even more than *Twilight Zone*. Form rejections. Sometimes I thought I could hear the assistant to the assistant editor's assistant's laughter when I opened that returned SASE.

There were many magazines that offered payment of about a penny per word. I'm pretty sure *The Horror Show* edited by David B. Silva fell into this category. I was a regular submitter to *The Horror Show* for a couple of reasons. First, it was a good magazine that published some amazing stories and I wanted to be part of that. But also because the editorial staff did more than a form letter. The half-size sheet of paper included a list of reasons my story was rejected. I don't have these anymore, so can't tell you all of the possibilities, but the checklist included things to tell the author about weak plots, poor character-ization, too many grammatical errors, that the magazine had already accepted something similar, etc. And there was a line for "Please try us again." That was always checked, and I took that as much-needed encouragement to keep bothering those poor people.

I never made it into *The Horror Show*, either.

After the magazines like *The Horror Show* that paid semi-profes-sional rates, there was the no-pay — or for-the-love — magazines, and these varied incredibly in quality. Some were mimeographed, folded, and saddle-stapled. Some where ... What's that? What is "mimeo-graphed"? In the days before the photocopier, there was a thing called a mimeograph machine in which the printer — a person — would use a master sheet he or she had made, and crank a handle on the machine to turn out copies reproduced in a blurry purple ink that retained a very specific and peculiar aroma that children who went to school after the 1970s probably never experienced.

My first acceptance was to a magazine I have never seen and can no longer remember the name of. It was edited by a guy who is still active in the genre as an author. He accepted my short story "Nocturnal Caress," but it was never published (and I was never paid because payment was made on publication). Remember that this is a book about failing as an author. My first acceptance was a failure for two reasons. The first is that the story was never published. The second is because I mailed my only copy of the story to the magazine (see the previous chapter about technology; I was writing on a typewriter and too poor to pay for photocopies).

In that version of the story, the little girl was eaten by the monster under her bed and her bloody foot was the only thing left for Mom to find. Losing that draft was probably a victory, because when I rewrote the story it was tamer, but also much better. I've read that story to high school students and at conventions many times and it's generally well received.

The first time I saw my name in print with a short story I wrote was in 1992 with the Halloween issue (Vol. #2, Issue #4) of *The Midnight Zoo*, one of those "for-the-love" magazines that didn't pay. They published good stories, though, and the magazine itself was of the same quality as, say, *The Horror Show*, with thick, full-color covers and normal paper for pages, not the pulpy newsprint paper of digests like *Night Cry*. My story was "Unholy Womb," a Halloween piece about an Illinois boy who discovers that Voodoo Charlie cursed all the pumpkin fields so that every pumpkin contained a little monster made of pulp and seeds that would attack and suck blood from people until the monster swelled and popped, then the head kept sucking until there was nothing left in the victim.

Vol. #2, Issue #4 of The Midnight Zoo featured my first published short story, "Unholy Womb."

With my grammar issues finally under control, I started placing stories in some of the no-pay magazines, and I was thrilled every time I got an acceptance and saw my published work. But I was still trying to get someone to pay me for something.

That finally happened with the January/February 1994 issue of *Terminal Fright* magazine, edited by Ken Abner. Ken accepted my weird Western horror story "A Drink from the Springs" and paid me half-a-cent per word. I got a check for $2.95. I thought I was on my way!

I was not. It would be many, many years before anyone paid me for another word of fiction.

Before I move on, I do have to mention one more for-the-love magazine that was of great benefit to me back in the day. *Mausoleum* was edited and published by "Crow Ravenscar" aka Kelly Ganson of New Mexico. She was the first to publish my werewolves when she accepted "Biological Clock" for her magazine. She went on to publish several of my stories and poems and gave me great advice on editing my sword-and-sorcery fantasy novel.

There were others, mostly of poorer quality, but done with love and the best the editors/publishers could do with their resources.

The late 1980s and early 1990s were an amazing time for horror fiction and movies. There were so many hungry markets for stories, and I was so frustrated that I wasn't able to tap into the paying markets. Looking back, I can see that I wasn't very good, but honestly, neither were some of the authors getting book deals with New York publishers.

The January/February 1994 issue of Terminal Fright magazine was the first time I got paid for fiction. It had my story "A Drink from the Springs" in its pages.

WHAT STORY WAS IN THIS?

Online 'Zines

With every boom comes a bust. The horror bubble burst in the early to mid-1990s. Most of the magazines I just mentioned went belly-up.

Horror movie releases dried to a trickle, and the genre became the butt of jokes.

But there were still a lot of us die-hards who soldiered on and found a new world opening up on the other side of our noisy computer modems.

The online magazines took over where the for-the-love print magazines had died. These new "e-zines" didn't cost anything to produce, provided the publisher knew a little bit of HTML coding. And even better, the author no longer had to go to the post office to submit stories because there was this new thing called electronic mail. The future was there!

By the end of the 1990s, my life had changed a lot. My career as a CNC machinist came to an end due to a work injury. Forced to do something else, I finally went to college, earning a bachelor's degree in journalism in 1999, at the age of 33. College, and then working as a newspaper reporter, drained me of creativity and I hardly wrote anything for a few years. However, it was a good time for me in terms of publishing short stories.

Two online markets stand out in my memory of that time. The first is *Short Scary Tales*, an online horror magazine published and edited by Englishman Paul Fry. Paul published several of my old stories that I'd never placed with print magazines. He held a contest at one point and my story "Reunion" won the readers' poll. The other e-zine was called *DeathGrip* and was managed by Walt Hicks. Paul, Walt, myself, and a few other authors became a sort of cabal for a while, and that felt good.

Nobody was making any money. Paul and Walt didn't pay for the stories, and nobody had really thought about buying or selling advertising in e-zines yet. But we were getting exposure. Yeah. Exposure.

The electric company doesn't take that in payment for the power to turn on a light bulb.

Paul Fry gave me my first book publication when he accepted my story "Dining at Sea" for his anthology *Cold Storage* in 2000 (after we all survived Y2K). Four years later, Walt Hicks and editing partner Terry "Horns" Erwin gave me my second anthology publication when *Death-Grip 3: It Came from the Cinema* included my story "Path of Pins," a story inspired by my reading of an old rendition of "Little Red Riding Hood" but surprisingly is not about werewolves. By that time, our little group was mostly broken up, the online publications dead and gone, and we all fell out of touch, but I have very fond memories of those few years when I could e-mail a story and see it up on a website where anyone anywhere in the world could come by and read it.

Short Scary Tales Publication's Cold Storage included my first anthology publication in 2000 with "Dining at Sea."

Later, online publications would come into their own, start making and paying money, giving readers "an advertising experience" and basically replace most print magazines.

Not everything about online publication was good, even during the good times. At some point, I came across a horror website that had a nice look and feel, had an editor who seemed to know her stuff, and she accepted reprints. So, my dumb ass sent her several old stories, including the three Halloween-themed stories I'd had published in print magazines. This, of course, included "Unholy Womb," my very first publication.

I learned a very hard lesson about online publication. The problem was that anyone could drag their mouse down the length of a story, then cut and paste that text into a word processor, a message board, or another website and reproduce the story without paying or notifying the creator, and could even delete the original author's name and substitute their own name.

This happened with "Unholy Womb." I don't remember what made me search for my own story online, but I did one day. I just typed the first sentence into a search engine ... and it came back with multiple hits. The story had been republished on other horror and Halloween websites. I found it pasted into the message board for the band Linkin Park. The worst, though, was finding that it had won a contest sponsored by a major software company, and that my story had been submitted under someone else's name. I spent days contacting people, telling them that was my story and they did not have permission to republish it. The software company basically told me "too bad, so sad" about the plagiarism. Most of the online magazines apologized and either asked permission or took the story down.

The website where I'd given permission for the stories to be republished had changed hands. Messages sent to the contact e-mail address went unanswered. I never got those stories taken down from the original site, but it did finally get shut down. "Unholy Womb," however, is still floating around the web on unauthorized sites. When I began self-publishing, one of the first books I released was *Unholy Womb and Other Halloween Tales*. Obviously, because "Unholy Womb" was my first published story, but also so that my book would come up in search engines if anyone looked for the story name.

After years and years of submitting stories that suffered from everything from poor grammar to ridiculous plots (yes, an editor told me that about an early version of "SKN-3") to "just not for us right now", I finally had a couple dozen short stories that had been published, all but one for no pay. And then I had a story that got popular and was stolen, republished without permission, and plagiarized.

Even amidst a tiny bit of success, I was still failing.

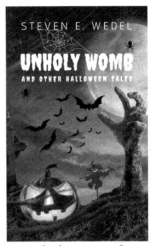

A fairly new cover for one of my first self-published collections, Unholy Womb and Other Halloween Tales

SMALL PRESSES

By the early 2000s, my short story well was drying up. When I earned my bachelor's degree in 1999 I had seven novel-length manuscripts completed. Four were horror stories, but one was fantasy, one was science fiction, and one was historical romance. Even then, I couldn't contain myself to one genre of fiction. Those novels were pretty bad, except for the last one about a young woman who becomes a werewolf.

I was pretty deep into the writing of *Shara* when I started attending classes at the University of Central Oklahoma in the fall of 1997. At first, I went as a non-degree-seeking student to take classes taught by their artist-in-residence, mystery writer Carolyn Wheat. Under her guidance, *Shara* became the best of my novel manuscripts, and my best chance at publication.

I submitted *Shara* over and over and over to agents and to every New York City major house that might even think about publishing a werewolf novel where the monster was the hero, similar to Anne Rice's *The Vampire Chronicles*. Agents, especially, wanted exclusive submissions back then, and I played by the rules for fear of getting multiple offers and the agents finding out I'd submitted to more than one at a time. What a joke! So, the wait between one submission, rejection, and the next submission was sometimes very, very long.

Because I wasn't working a full-time job, I took heavy loads of college classes and finished my four-year degree in three years. *Shara* was on submission somewhere most of that time, and for a few years after I graduated. In fact, my career as a journalist came and went and I'd sold my soul to corporate America before my first novel ever got accepted for publication.

At some point in 1998 or 1999, I almost fell into one of the oldest traps out there for writers. You have to remember that the internet was not what it is today. You couldn't just sit down and research something. There was no Writer Beware website listing scams and shady dealers. So, I submitted *Shara* to Northwest Publishing, Inc. and, to my utter shock and disbelief, someone from the company called to say they wanted to publish my book.

Glory hallelujah! It was finally about to happen!

Except this is a book about failing, so you know it certainly was *not* about to happen.

The person on the other end of the phone was a smooth talker. My book would be available to every bookstore. It would have a full-color cover and be in a popular trade paperback format, blah blah blah. He'd send me the contract and a sample of one of their books by FedEx and I'd have it tomorrow.

He did. I did. And I read the contract, which is probably something he hoped I wouldn't do because, you see, Northwest Publishing, Inc. was a vanity press. They weren't going to pay me. They wanted *me* to pay *them*! Then they'd send me a bunch of books I could try to convince bookstores to stock and sell.

It shames me a little to admit to you how much I considered their offer.

There was a voice in my head telling me this was not the right thing to do. My heart begged for it because I wanted to see my name on the cover of a book so badly. My wife agreed with the voice in my head. I also remembered an episode of *The Waltons* TV show where John Boy got a box of books and a bill for their printing, which was really all I knew about vanity presses prior to this experience.

In the end, I didn't do it. It was heartbreaking, but it was one of the rare times I made the right decision.

Not to fear, though. I was about to learn there was a new thing called "print on demand" and there were new scams and other problems associated with that new technology.

The Bad

The year was 2001 and I was a writer in Conoco Inc.'s human resources department. I'd relocated my family to Ponca City, Oklahoma, and was earning more money than I'd ever made before. My wife stopped complaining that she still had to work after all the expense associated with me going to college and she got to stay home with our new baby and the two older kids.

My new job was mind-numbingly boring. I came to it from the state's biggest daily newspaper, where I consistently led the newsroom in the number of bylines earned each month. I'd turn out three or four stories per day at the newspaper. At the new job, I was given articles to write about health insurance and retirement plans and I'd knock them out in a day or two. Finally, a co-worker came to me and said my new boss didn't know what to do with me because she expected it to take me weeks to write a newsletter, not a couple of days.

So, I rearranged my office to where my computer screen was not visible from the open door and worked on my fiction. I liked my co-workers, but I'm not sure I could have worked there until retirement. It didn't matter, thanks to corporate greed. The CEO sold Conoco to Phillips and Phillips shut down our department, so that job — and it's high salary — went away as quickly as it had come.

But I digress. The year was 2001 and I heard about a new publisher that was accepting manuscripts. Despite my eagerness, I was hesitant about this company I'd never heard of and didn't want to send them my best work, *Shara*. They were open to short story collections, so instead I collected all my previously published stories, plus a few others that I felt just needed a bit of polishing, and sent them the manuscript, which I named *Darkscapes*.

The book was accepted, and I joined the stable of authors with this new company called Publish America.

I didn't realize how crowded that stable was, nor that most of the authors stabled there were, well … not thoroughbreds. Not until the next year when *Darkscapes* was released.

The cover of the Publish America release of Dark-scapes.

By 2002, I'd used my high salary to join the Horror Writers Association as an affiliate member and I far too often waded into the toxic swamp of the HWA message board. I was still young enough and naive enough to believe I could convince strangers on the internet to change their minds if I just used a strong enough argument. Yeah, right.

HWA members had heard of Publish America, and the overall opinion was not favorable. PA was "a back door vanity press," according to the general consensus. This meant that, unlike Northwest Publishing Inc. that wanted me to pay up front for a load of books no bookstore wanted to sell, Publish America printed one book at a time at a price that was about $5 more than a comparable book from a traditional publisher.

Despite *Darkscapes* having a retail price of $19.95, I defended Publish America because, hey, they put my book in print. Led by one repugnant troll I've mentioned already and still won't name, the attacks against me, Publish America, and a few other members with books published by them were nasty and merciless and made me wonder why I had wanted to join HWA for so many years.

The only good that ever came from my publication with Publish America or HWA was finding a couple of other Oklahoma City-based horror authors, multi-Bram Stoker Award-winner Brian A. Hopkins, and fellow Publish America alum Jason Light. If I hadn't had books to sell, I'm not sure we would have met despite living in the same city.

I eventually got out of my contract with Publish America, but not before a couple more embarrassing incidents.

Brian, Jason, and I did some book signings together. The first one, at OKC-based independent seller Full Circle Books, was a huge success for me. I sold every copy of *Darkscapes* I had on hand, even at the ridiculously high price. Our second one was at a Borders store in Tulsa where, for whatever reason, my books didn't arrive. There I was with no books. The manager named a drink special in honor of *Darkscapes* for the day, but I didn't pocket any cash over that.

And then the greedy bastard running Conoco sold the company to another Oklahoma energy company, Phillips Petroleum, and suddenly I was jobless and looking for work. I applied for a copy editor position with a daily newspaper in Waco, Texas, and was asked to come down for an interview. While I was there, one of the interviewers told me he'd bought a copy of my book and the opening section was labeled "Forward" instead of "Foreword." Needless to say, I didn't get that job.

If you don't know the story, Google what the Science Fiction Writers of America did to expose Publish America. That happened after I got released from my contract. Despite all the negativity about Publish America, I will say they let me out of that contract without any kind of a fight. Still, it was a hard lesson ... and I wasn't done learning yet.

The Less Bad

We've arrived at a point in the narrative where I have to decide whether or not to name names. I'm going to straddle a middle ground and name the company names, but leave out the names of the people who ran them if what I have to say is mostly negative. Sadly, most of it is negative.

In early 2003 I submitted my darling *Shara* to yet another small press genre publisher. I can't remember the name of the company, though I do remember the publisher's name. There was an assistant editor/publisher who wanted to branch out on her own and asked me if she could make *Shara* one of the first releases for her new company, 3F Publications. I was thrilled with her enthusiasm and readily agreed.

The woman in charge, I believe, had good intentions from beginning to end. She signed me and a couple of other authors, one of whom was already an established name and another who was a debut novelist but has since gone on to some renown. I think she also published an anthology with upper mid-list names. But, it was all doomed.

She sent me a cover mock-up for *Shara*. I wasn't thrilled with it, but I gave it the okay. The cover had a black background with the title at the top and my name at the bottom, both in red Papyrus font (which I happen to like). In the middle was an inset picture of a very CGI naked woman with her tits and bits strategically covered by foliage and a wolf howling in the fog behind her. It was a decent cover for a print-on-demand book at the time.

When I got my author copies, the black background and Papyrus font were gone. The CGI image was stretched to fill the six-by-nine inch cover, making the naked brunette much more prominent, and distorted. It was bad. The publisher told me the printer wouldn't accept the original font and she had to make changes. I never learned why she didn't just change the font or why she stretched the image to fill the cover.

I only have this very low quality version of what the 3F Publications' edition of Shara was supposed to be.

The altered and unapproved cover 3F Publications used when Shara was published.

Then she debuted her company, along with multiple copies of all the books she'd published, at the Horrorfind convention in Hunt Valley, Maryland, in late 2003. She had a nice table in a heavily trafficked area and loads of books. What the table lacked was somebody to man it and take people's money. I heard later that she'd gotten a bad medical diagnosis just before the convention and she spent most of the con drunk in her hotel room. I don't know if that's true, but I do know I sat at her table much more than she did.

Here's a picture of me (in the OU cap) at the 3F Publications table with Gary A. Braunbeck having a conversation with Dallas Mayr, aka Jack Ketchum. I was so close to greatness there, and yet so far away. In a funny side note, I bought that cap to give to the publisher as an Oklahoma souvenir, but since I hardly saw her, I just kept it. Now, twenty-one years later, it is faded to almost pink, except where it is nearly black with sweat stains. It's disgusting, but still my favorite hat.

Me signing books with Gary A. Braunbeck at the 3F Publications table at the Horrorfind convention in 2003.

Needless to say, 3F Publications went out of business soon after that. I haven't heard from the publisher since 2004. I still believe her heart was in the right place and I hope she's doing well.

When *Shara* came out, I was back in Oklahoma City and briefly back in the world of journalism, working for *The Journal Record* newspaper. They ran a story about my upcoming novel release. The photographer asked me if I'd heard of Katherine Cross, the Oklahoma girl "murdered by human wolves" in 1917. I had not, but after some hurried research, I put together a novella called *Murdered by Human Wolves* and 3F Publications' owner wanted to release it as a chapbook to people who bought *Shara* at Horrorfind and through the Shock-lines online bookstore.

I built the chapbook myself using Microsoft Publisher and printed three or four copies with a cardstock cover featuring a photo of Cross's grave marker. The publisher said she'd take care of the rest. Obviously, that never happened. Of the copies I made, I still have one. I'm not sure what happened to the others.

Enter Scrybe Press, whose owner read and liked *Shara* and was interested in publishing me. With *Murdered by Human Wolves* not getting any kind of release by 3F, I offered it to Scrybe Press, and it was accepted. As with 3F and Publish America, there was no advance against royalties offered by Scrybe Press. The publisher got coveted artist GAK to do a pen-and-ink sketch for the saddle-stapled release of *MbHW* and it sold so well that Scrybe had to switch the book over to a print-on-demand trade paperback with new full-color artwork by Kirk Alberts.

"Murdered by human wolves"

Steven E. Wedel

The very, very limited edition of the prototype for Murdered by Human Wolves.

Scrybe Press published a chapbook edition of Murdered by Human Wolves with cover art by GAK.

Meanwhile, I got the rights back to *Shara* and gave the book to Scrybe Press for a reprint. Kirk did the artwork for the new edition. Kirk, by the way, is amazing. I love all five covers he's done for me.

Once again, and not for the last time, I'll remind you this is a book about failing as an author. Scrybe Press published *Murdered by Human Wolves, Shara, Seven Days in Benevolence*, and *Ulrik*. In all that time, I received one payment for royalties on *MbHW*. By the time I began writing *Nadia's Children*, I was insistently nagging the publisher for money and sales figures. Although he hadn't paid me, I was still under the delusion that I had to honor my agreement to give him first refusal on all books in The Werewolf Saga, which is why I killed almost everybody at the end of *Nadia's Children*.

I contacted the Better Business Bureau in New York, the chamber of commerce in the town where Scrybe Press was, and complained openly on message boards and that new thing called Facebook. Finally, the publisher's wife made a cash settlement with me and I got all my rights back and Scrybe Press died off.

But I wasn't done killing small presses. Oh no. Graveside Tales was next. The publisher wanted to do another release of my werewolf books, and did release a new edition of *Murdered by Human Wolves*. But then he wanted to break the other full novels into three chapbooks each, for a total of nine. I was against that because of the cost to readers.

I hadn't signed anything for those books, so I refused ... and then Graveside Tales went out of business.

Stonethread Publishing had been going for a while and I liked the way their books looked. Granted, the company mostly published the work of its owner, Harvey Stanbrough, but he published other people, too. He agreed to publish my first thriller, *Inheritance*. He did the layout, designed the cover, had the book in multiple e-reader formats, and then ... he decided Stonethread would exclusively publish only his own work. Despite some disappointment, I have nothing but good things to say about Harvey. He gave me all the text and cover files for my book. By this time, I was already self-publishing my Werewolf Saga books under my own MoonHowler Press imprint, so I was able to take his work and publish *Inheritance* myself. Harvey later helped me improve my cover design for *A Light Beyond*. Stonethread Publishing is still going, but my book was the last he prepared before closing to outside submissions.

Somewhere in all this, my friend Craig Wolf told me about Fine Tooth Press, a publisher of all genres and the publisher of his first two books. I sent the publisher a revamped version of *Darkscapes* where I pulled the three stories I felt were weakest and replaced them with three newer ones. He published the book. I hated the cover. I mean, I *HATED* the cover, which featured a fat Asian man's face with a messed up eyeball and everything tinted green. WTF? No advance against royalties. No payment. Ever. No communication from the publisher after a short time. The book was published in 2006. I found out in 2023 the publisher had died several years ago.

Harvey Stanbrough designed the cover for Inheritance when he was initially going to publish the book through his Stonethread Publishing.

The awful Fine Tooth Press cover of the 2nd edition of Darkscapes.

Do you want more? I've got it. Let's talk about Bad Moon Books, a prestigious small press that had books that won Stoker Awards. I was over the bad moon when Roy Robbins, the publisher, decided to accept my novella *Little Graveyard on the Prairie*. Roy did a line of novellas in limited release, and he paid up front for them. So, yes, I got paid, and I got my first hardcover publication. *Little Graveyard on the Prairie* was released in a special lettered edition, and a lesser hardcover numbered edition of, I think, 200 copies. They didn't sell out because, hey, I'm not a popular author.

Roy accepted the next thing I sent him, my graduate thesis novel *Amara's Prayer*. He told me the ending made his editor cry. He released the book ... and then promptly closed down Bad Moon Books so he could go to seminary. I can't fault him for that, but damn! The timing, ya know?

The cover of the numbered hardcover edition of Little Graveyard on the Prairie, published by Bad Moon Books.

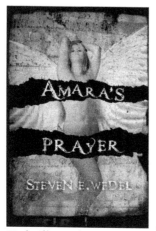

Kirk Alberts' glorious cover for my novel Amara's Prayer from Bad Moon Books.

Double Dragon Publishing released an e-book version of *Seven Days in Benevolence*. They had it available for years. I never saw a dime before I requested the rights be returned.

Permuted Press was one of the top small genre presses, specializing in zombie novels and anthologies. I read that they were branching out, so I sent them my manuscript *The Prometheus Syndrome*, which has a zombie in it. They not only accepted my novel, but wanted to sign me to a three-book deal. Yes! This time has to be it, right! Wrong. The original owner that made the company so respectable sold it and the new owners were only publishing e-books unless the electronic version was really selling, then they'd do a trade paperback. No advance, and I knew enough by this time to know they weren't going to promote me and I wasn't going to make any money, so I backed out of the deal.

That was the last time I submitted a book to a small press.

Lessons from the Small Press

The first fifteen years of the new millennium were frustrating in terms of publications. New technology opened new frontiers, but that simply opened the way for more author scams and more chances for people who loved books but had no business sense to hurt their own reputations and the careers of aspiring writers.

I learned a lot from the experience I gained. I also got some really cool book covers, some of which I'm still able to use.

Also, for a brief time, it seemed as though I was poised to take that next step. My Werewolf Saga was pretty popular for being a small press series with very little promotional force behind it. Word of mouth was very good. I was "the werewolf guy" in horror circles for a while and even Gary Brandner, author of *The Howling* trilogy, praised *Shara* on a message board. I had blurbs from Gary A. Braunbeck, Tom Piccirilli, and Brian Keene, plus good reviews at reputable horror websites.

But I was never able to take that next step. Publishers failed. My income was severely cut and I wasn't able to continue going to major conventions, so I lost most of my contacts in the genre. Then I started branching out and publishing in other genres.

You likely will have bad experiences, too. You can't let them get you down. If you're meant to write, you have to do it. You won't be able to stop. Learn from my mistakes. Learn from your mistakes, bad decisions, bad luck, or whatever, and keep pounding those keys and looking ahead.

Once again, remember that money flows TO the writer. If you're asked to pay, stay away. And if they're not paying you up front, they're not going to pay to promote your book.

LITERARY AGENTS

If you want to publish in the big leagues, you really must have a literary agent. Most of the major publishing houses won't even look at your manuscript unless it comes to them through a literary agent that they've actually heard of. Why? Because if a trusted literary agent brings the book to the publisher, it tells the publisher that the work is at least good enough that a reputable agent wants to represent it.

Getting an agent is no easy feat in itself.

I don't currently have a literary agent, but I have had three of them at various times in the past. I'm only going to identify them by first name in this chapter. In the case of the first one, the relationship ended in an ugly way between me and the woman who took over the agency ... if you can even call it that. With another, I'm making some speculations about why the relationship didn't work and I might be wrong, though evidence seems to support my hypothesis.

Impersonating Competency

After attending my first Horrorfind convention in 2003, I was put in contact with a woman named Jane who called herself a literary agent. It was another author who brought us together, but I can't remember now who that was. I wish I could because I'd sure like to compare notes, but whatever. Incompetent doesn't begin to describe Jane. Let me tell you about this short relationship.

First, not long after I signed on with her, I learned that she'd been at that Horrorfind convention and had offered oral sex to some male authors who had already established themselves in the genre if they'd let her represent them. I never received such an offer, and I don't know of any author who claimed that benefit.

As I said in the previous chapter, 3F Publications fell apart right after that convention, so my novel *Shara* was in a limbo. Jane was supposed to help me find it a new home. I don't think she ever read it. She disappeared for a long time, then reappeared with no explanation, and still didn't seem to be doing anything for me.

Then I heard through the grapevine that a producer named Brendan was looking for a werewolf property for a very well known director of one of the biggest horror movie franchises of the day. So I contacted Jane and asked that she send Brendan my novel. She required I send her two copies, which I did. She assured me she'd sent one to the producer. I never heard anything.

Then Jane disappeared again. She was in a psych ward. I don't know what happened, but apparently that's where she'd been the last time she stopped responding to e-mails, too. A bitch I knew from the HWA message board, who happened to be friends with Jane, stepped in to run the so-called agency. We clashed again immediately. I got an e-mail from Brian Keene telling me I needed to log in to some message board where this woman ranted about me. Jane was supposed to have sent

Shara to Tor Books. Her replacement claimed to have connections at Tor and that I would *never* be published by Tor.

The replacement ended my association with Jane's agency and returned all my material, which included the two copies of *Shara*, one of which Jane said she had sent to Brendan. Not long after, that famous director released a real stinker of a teenybopper werewolf movie.

Thus ended my first partnership with a literary agent.

The next one wasn't as tempestuous, but it was just as disappointing. I found an agent named Lantz listed somewhere and among his very, very limited client list was the name of a female horror author I knew of but had never met. Her debut novel was schedule to be released by Tor Books. I contacted the author and asked, "Did Lantz take care of your contract with Tor Books?" She told me yes, he had. He only wanted to represent Southern writers, and he was interested in whatever book it was I was pitching at the time. He'd made a deal with a publisher I wanted to work with, so I signed with him.

Semantics, my dear reader. Semantics are so important. Lantz never sold a word I wrote. Later, I contacted that female author again to see if she could enlighten me on why I wasn't getting anywhere with Lantz. Turns out, he was good with contracts, but he had no connections in the industry. The author had pitched, submitted, and gotten an offer from Tor, then hired Lantz to handle the contract negotiations.

I fired him. I can't say if he ever even submitted anything I sent him. He said he did, but I never saw any proof of it. I haven't heard anything from or about him since our relationship ended.

The Dream Agency

Third time is a charm, right? It kind of was. There's a whole back story here that I'm going to save for the next chapter. For now, just know that I met Carrie Jones at Conestoga, a science fiction convention that used to be held annually in Tulsa, Oklahoma. That was in 2009. At the time, Carrie had two young adult novels published, with a third due very soon. None of them were horror or had any supernatural elements to them, but she'd placed her fourth book, called *Need*, with Bloomsbury and it had werewolves and pixies in it.

Carrie and I were paired together for a speed-date-the-author event at the convention. We went from table to table meeting fans who had signed up to participate. We hit it off right away. If you've read her blog or watched one of her many podcasts, you know that she's a funny, quirky, smart woman, and she's not acting for an online persona. That's the real Carrie.

After the speed-dating event, we went to the bar and continued to talk. We have daughters the same age. We like werewolves. We got along great, and so naturally we said we should work on something together. After the convention, we stayed in touch via e-mail, and pretty soon we had a very rough idea for a novel.

In less than a month, we wrote a long young adult novel we called *Ghost Sickness*.

Carrie's agent, Edward, didn't like the idea of her writing a book with some no-name small press author from Oklahoma. Since we did it, though, he agreed to take me on as a client, though he tried to get Carrie to claim a bigger cut of any money made from our collaboration. Because Carrie is Carrie, she refused to do that.

Now, there's something you have to know at this point. I believe John Steinbeck is America's greatest author. Period. Better than Mark Twain. Better than Ernest Hemingway, William Faulkner, or anybody else you want to throw in the ring. Edward worked for the agency that represented Steinbeck for his entire career. I had a New York City literary agent. Not just any agent, but one that worked for the agency that represented my literary hero. He told me they had drawers with Steinbeck's actual handwritten manuscripts. How does one even function with such a holy relic in the building? I was shitting in the tallest of cotton! And this was before he even sold the book.

Edward did, indeed, sell what became *After Obsession* to Bloomsbury for a five-figure deal, and he sold foreign language rights in several other countries. I'll talk more about the book and the publishing experience in the next chapter. Based on the success of that deal, I wrote my first solo young adult supernatural novel and sent it to Edward.

He didn't like my title, *The Girls Nobody Wanted to Date*. I changed it to *Love Curse*. Based on his advice, I made major revisions twice. Still, he told me he didn't think he could sell it.

Around this time, Edward changed jobs and went to another agency, so my literary connection to the estate of John Steinbeck was severed. I was pretty disappointed by that, but still, Edward was a known commodity.

I sent him my new solo young adult book called *Afterlife*, a post-apocalyptic story about a boy who could see the ghosts of people killed when an asteroid collided with Earth and knocked the planet off its axis. Prior to the disaster, the boy's father, a policeman who was also a doomsday prepper, had been killed during a traffic stop. Edward wanted me to write a book about the boy's relationship with his father. I wasn't interested in that as anything more than a bit of back story to the novel I'd written.

I fired Edward. You have to understand that I'm not one to end a relationship, no matter how bad it is. I didn't want to end that one, but it had become obvious that he was not going to represent my solo work, so I had to walk away.

Later, after she also ended her professional partnership with him, Carrie told me that Edward had been less than thrilled when she wrote

Need. It seems he just didn't like supernatural fiction, and at the time that was all I wrote.

Carrie and I wrote another novel together. Okay, actually, as of this writing, we've written four novels together, but only two are currently published. She had a new agent named Erin. As with Edward, Erin took me on as a client, but specified it was only for the one book with Carrie and that she was not my agent for anything else unless I went through the usual submission process and she accepted it, which she didn't. She did, however, broker a deal for the book that became *In the Woods* with (listen up, Jane's friend) Tor Books.

The Right Fit

So, here I am without an agent. Do I want an agent? Sure. I'd like to have an agent and score big book contracts. I'd gladly give the agent his or her 15 percent of the take to get me with a big New York City publisher. But this is a book about failing as an author.

Like I did with Publish America and 3F Publications, I jumped at the chance to work with my first two agents despite them having virtually no track record, not communicating, not showing me any evidence they were doing what they claimed. I was desperate. Authors need agents. I probably would have signed with a chimpanzee wearing a Simon and Schuster T-shirt if he'd nodded his head at me.

I stayed with all three of my agents longer than I should have. With all three, there were signs that the relationship wasn't going anywhere positive.

Business partnerships are like marriages. The partners have to have the same goal, the same desire, the same drive, and work together like horses in harness, or it just won't work. And like a marriage that's not working, it can be a difficult breakup when the time comes.

Don't jump on shady publishing deals, and don't sign with an agent until you know his or her track record and talk to at least two clients about their relationship with the agent. You, the author, are paying the agent. Not up front. Don't ever do that! But if the agent sells your book, the publisher's check will go to the agent, who will take his or her cut before sending the rest to you. Make sure you are getting everything you pay for.

MAJOR PUBLISHERS

When I sat down to write this book, I knew it was going to focus on mistakes I made along the way and close calls where I should have found success, but didn't. This chapter about major publishers will be short because my experience is limited in that regard. What I have to say isn't all positive, but don't be fooled, I would love to work with a major publisher for the rest of my life if that was an option.

I talked a little about my collaborations with Carrie Jones in the previous chapter about agents. The only books issued by major publishers to bear my name on the cover are the two I co-authored with Carrie. All my other experience with New York publishers has been rejections, usually in the way of form letters. Obviously, my experience is not the experience of everyone working with the big houses. Hopefully, my experience is just another anomaly unique to me and my brand of luck.

After Obsession

So, back in 2009 I met Carrie in Tulsa. In 2010 we completed our first book, which we called *Ghost Sickness*. We wrote that sucker in less than a month, e-mailing the Microsoft Word file back and forth. It was a blast! We only had the barest of outlines, so we didn't know specifics of what was going to happen next. It was like a choose-your-own-adventure story, and we'd try to create bigger and bigger cliffhangers at the end of our chapters for each other to deal with. So much fun!

It was so much fun that the original finished draft came in at 102,000 words.

The book tells the story of Alan, a half-Navajo high school student from Oklahoma City, who has to move to a small town in Maine after his uncle goes missing at sea. His mom needs to support her sister. Alan has a cousin named Courtney, who is a year younger and is best friends with Aimee, who has a jerk of a boyfriend. Yada, yada, yada, Courtney becomes possessed by a demon from the nearby river and Alan and Aimee have to perform a kinda sorta Navajo exorcism on her. There we go, a young adult horror novel.

It made sense that the story begin with Alan because he was the one undergoing the most change right off. That's what we did. The editor at Bloomsbury, however, said that the audience for paranormal romances is girls, so the book should open with the female perspective. Okay, fine.

Then they wanted to change the title. Ghost sickness is the English translation of the term the Navajo people call demonic possession. Plus, it's just a cool title. Bloomsbury changed it to *After Obsession*. I told them then, and I stand by it now, that name sounds like a knockoff perfume brand. This was really my first indication that we had sold our baby for filthy lucre.

The money was nice. I can't speak for Carrie, but I made more money off the advance against royalties for *After Obsession* than anything I've written, ever. Since they laid out so much cash for the book, Bloomsbury's editorial team got to call the shots. That's how the game works.

Next came the cuts. Maybe the book had a little fat that needed trimming. Okay. But they turned Leatherface loose on the pages. Remember, Carrie had published paranormal books, but I was the horror author, and I wrote a lot of the scariest scenes in what became *After Obsession* ... and the editor didn't like them. They were too intense for the teenage audience.

Remember that I was a high school English teacher at the time. It was 2011. The kids I was teaching gobbled up the gore and loved it. I don't think the original scenes were too graphic for the audience of that time. The post-covid kids? Yeah. Words and images hurt them. But, whatever. Readers didn't get to see possessed Courtney with leaking acne going through the lunch line, pointing at random students and telling their nasty secrets.

The cover reveal of the novel was a big deal. I'll tell you, it's a gorgeous cover for a young adult paranormal novel. The title is in a fancy blue font with curlycues. There's a teenage girl in a strapless dress levitating with darkness dripping from her dress to the bottom of the cover. The cover of a book is meant to get the reader's attention, and this one did. Never mind that nobody ever put on a fancy dress or levitated in the story.

The hardback cover image of After Obsession, written with Carrie Jones and published by Bloomsbury.

When *After Obsession* was finally published in 2012, the book was down to 76,300 words. That's a cut of over 25,000 words for those of you who don't want to do the math.

Reviewers didn't comment on the book being cut by over 25,000 words, because, of course, they didn't know. What they roasted the book for was the "insta-love" between Aimee and Alan. There had been a lot of character development and little events that led up to Aimee dumping her jerk boyfriend while getting to know Alan, but a ton of that was hacked out of the story, so it does read like Aimee saw the hot Indian dude with long hair and looked for a reason to ditch the guy who was the star athlete before Alan showed up.

On a funny side note, at least one reviewer on YouTube talked about how obvious it was that Carrie and I had our own romance going. We'd met in person only once before writing the book, lived 2,000 miles from each other and, oh yeah, were both married to other people. As we'll see later, people often make up their own stories about authors and their books, but it isn't always funny like this one was.

So, just before the novel was released, the editor we'd been working with on *After Obsession* left Bloomsbury for another job. Her replacement hadn't bought the book, and therefore didn't have the enthusiasm for the book, and so didn't push it as hard as she would have if it had been her book. Twelve years later, with a trade paperback release after the hardcover, *After Obsession* still hasn't earned out the advance we were given against royalties.

For those of you who aren't writers, you're probably asking if that means we had to pay some of the money back. No, it was the publisher's loss. But it meant they weren't going to be interested in losing more money on a follow-up. We'll get to that in a minute.

Something really big had happened between that Conestoga event where I met Carrie and the release of our first book together. One of us had become a *New York Times* best-selling author. Based on the title of this book, you should already know that somebody was not me. Carrie's novel *Need* did pretty well as a hardcover from Bloomsbury. But when the sequel, *Captivate*, came out in hardcover and *Need* in paperback, both became bestsellers. It couldn't have happened to a nicer gal!

Carrie reached those lofty heights about a year before *After Obsession* was released. I was her co-author on this new novel! People were going to *love* it and want to know who this guy was who was writing with their favorite *New York Times* bestselling author. Right? Wrong. I really thought at least my Werewolf Saga books would see an increase in sales, but they didn't.

Reviewers either praised Carrie or criticized her for the book. I was barely mentioned.

In the Woods

By the time the hardcover of *After Obsession* hit bookstores, we'd already begun working on plans for more collaborative novels, so the magic could still happen, I believed.

In the Woods was originally called *Summer Howl*, a working title that neither of us liked, but neither of us could come up with a suitable title. Our eventual editor and her team named the novel, and I think they did okay with it.

That editor was not at Bloomsbury. The *After Obsession* contract gave Bloomsbury first right of refusal for our next collaboration, and that's just what they did, refuse it. Of course, what we pitched wasn't the book that became *In the Woods*, but a sequel to *After Obsession*, something we're still interested in writing someday, though it may never happen because of a rights issue, and time.

In *After Obsession*, the boy from Oklahoma (where I live) traveled to Maine (where Carrie lives). For the next book, we reversed that. Logan lives on a ranch with his very traditional family, Mom and Dad and two younger sisters. One night while lying in a field writing bad love poems, he hears a noise and gets to see a dark shape rip the head off a calf. Local papers and tabloids call it a Bigfoot sighting, and that gets the attention of a divorced kindergarten teacher and amateur cryptozoologist in Maine, who brings his teenage daughter to Oklahoma to investigate. Chrystal and Logan meet, and it seems the monster attacks are focused around Chrystal, so naturally he has to help protect her. Yada, yada, yada, they fall in love while devising and executing a plan to kill the monster.

One of my favorite things about this book was the monster. Everyone assumed it was a Bigfoot. However, through Chrystal's father, we revealed that Bigfoot is really a werewolf. Nobody's found Bigfoot skeletons in the woods, but human skeletons are found all the time. That's because when a werewolf dies, it transforms back into its human form. Carrie and I both had series featuring werewolves with very specific, and incompatible, mythologies, so we had to come up with new rules for the werewolf in this book. As with *After Obsession*, we sent the file back and forth, not really knowing what was going to happen next and trying to up the stakes with each cliffhanger.

Our agent sold the novel to Tor Books. Tor didn't pay us as much as Bloomsbury did, but it was still a lot of money, which was great, because my last payment came as my marriage broke up and I really needed the cash right then.

I much preferred working with Tor over Bloomsbury. Our editor cut out very little compared to the previous book, left the structure as we'd had it, leading with the boy's point of view, and just seemed to care more about our opinion of her feedback and suggestions. It was a good experience.

It took a lot longer for *In the Woods* to be released after it was accepted. During that time, I pitched my young adult post-apocalyptic novel *Afterlife* to our editor. She agreed to look at it, but said it might take a while. *In the Woods* wasn't released until 2019, by the way. The wheels moved slowly at Tor. I think it was five years between acceptance and publication. But that's not the point. The editor had *Afterlife* for years. I'd nag her every once in a while, until finally she rejected it. Why? The post-apocalyptic trend was winding down. Another swing and another miss.

Guess what. The same thing that happened with our editor at Blooms-bury happened at Tor. She left us to become a freelance editor. Welcome, New Editor Who Didn't Fall In Love With Our Book. Very little push upon release, the advance was never earned, and Tor Books passed on the two se-quels we'd written for *In the Woods*.

But this time being the co-author with a *New York Times* bestselling au-thor lifted my career and my other books started selling like ice water in Hell, right? I mean, they left the scary

In the Woods, written with Carrie Jones and published by Tor Books.

stuff intact for *In the Woods*, so readers wanted more horror, right? Right?

No.

The reviews I saw for *In the Woods* were generally better than *After Obsession*, but there weren't nearly as many of them. And again, Carrie got the credit and the blame.

Two novels with a *New York Times* bestselling co-author and my backlist received no CPR as a result. And I couldn't sell my solo work, even when I wrote in the first person present tense that is so popular in YA and rather difficult for me.

But it was a great learning experience. I learned a lot about different styles of editing and got to see the behind-the-scenes reasons some books get negative reviews. I got to see the complexities of a contract with a real major publishing house. I saw just how painfully slow the process of publishing in New York City can be.

Mostly, I learned how much artistic control the author gives up for those big paychecks. And how easy it is for the editor who took that control to just walk away from what she'd done. I'm not knocking either of those ladies for taking better opportunities. It's simply the way the world works. It just kinda sucked for us.

If I ever have the opportunity to work with a big-time publisher offering a big advance, you better believe I'll probably jump at it, but I'll go in with my eyes open, knowing that, first, I won't get all that money right up front and that it might be years between the first payment and the next, as well as between acceptance and release. And I'll know that I very likely will be asked to cut lines, scenes, and maybe chapters that I think are necessary.

Imagine having a baby and some executive in a suit walks in and says, "I might be able to make your baby a big success if you'll sign here." He offers you a contract, then says, "Your baby doesn't need both of those arms to be a success" then pulls out a machete and ... Well, you get the idea.

In my experience, working with the major publishers is a choice between high pay and artistic freedom. Which one will you choose?

GOING INDIE

My publishing company, MoonHowler Press, came into existence in 2001 when I created a werewolf sampler chapbook named *Call to the Hunt* that I sent along with paper submissions of *Shara* to New York City publishers. Yes, I did that. Don't do that. I used the name on all my self-made promotional material for the next dozen years.

With the collapse of Scrybe Press and disagreements about the way to release my Werewolf Saga novels at Graveside Tales, I made the decision to step into the arena of self publishing for real and signed up with Amazon.com's two services, CreateSpace for paperbacks and Kindle Direct Publishing (KDP) for e-books. Amazon has since merged the two under the KDP banner. Using Amazon's templates and the very temperamental MS Word, I formatted my paperbacks' interiors. If you have never done this, let me tell you that Word is an absolute bitch to work with when it comes to page numbering different sections of your book.

For covers, I had my oldest son, Alex, create covers for *Shara, Ulrik,* and my first brand-new release, *Nadia's Children*. He had taken a graphic design course at the vocational school affiliated with his high school. I think he did a good job, and I got a lot of compliments on his design at signing events.

The first three volumes of The Werewolf Saga with covers by my son, Alex Wedel.

For *Shara*, which you'll recall had already been published twice, I went back to material I'd worked up in a writing class in around 1993 and added that into the novel. These were the scenes were Shara was at the scene of a bank robbery and was working nights in the insurance office. Maybe a couple of others that I can't recall right now. It added character development before she turns into a horny, slobbering monster. Or it just makes the beginning more boring. I don't know.

To make my publishing venture feel legitimate, I worked up a simple MoonHowler Press logo using clipart I found online. With this on the spine, I was ready to go and MoonHowler Press was in the arena of "independent publishers," which just meant I was self-publishing under a company name, of course. At the time, though, Amazon allowed indie authors to include a publisher name on both print and e-book releases. Now, they only allow that on e-books, with the book information on their site listing paperbacks as "Independently Published."

MoonHowler Press

The original Moon-Howler Pres logo made from free clipart.

MoonHowler Press released a lot of books from me and my two pseudonyms over the next nine years. All of them were on Amazon, and all of them were enrolled in Kindle Unlimited, meaning reader-members could download them for free and I got paid based on the number of pages the user actually read.

I wasn't getting rich, and that, my friends, was a problem.

Wide vs. Exclusive

One of the issues with Amazon's KU program is that the author has to agree to only publish the books through KDP. That means my books weren't available to Barnes and Noble customers, or Kobo's, or to libraries and a host of other retailers and venues.

Also, the internet is full of horror stories about authors having their entire KDP account shut down because a bot misread something, and appeals are not always easy or successful.

Then I heard about this concept called "going wide." It turns out, there were alternatives to Amazon's KDP. I read about an aggregator called Draft2Digital where I could upload my books once and they'd be available to multiple outlets that Amazon didn't reach.

Hell yeah, brother!

I began pulling my books from KU in late 2022 and uploading them to D2D as fast as the KU agreements ended. Now, I didn't take them down from Amazon's KDP because Amazon has some specific criteria that has to be met and, while D2D does have an option to create Kindle books, it's just better to upload directly to KDP. As long as you avoid Kindle Unlimited, you're perfectly fine in doing this.

Draft2Digital bought up Smashwords not long after I joined them. I'd published through Smashwords earlier and didn't care for it. Their guidelines were draconian and I never had many sales, so I'd pretty much abandoned them. Now, D2D has sales events directly linked to Smashwords. Because I'm not good at math and sometimes don't read the fine print, I often take part and end up giving books away for free and don't even get bad reviews in exchange. If you agree to participate, make sure you look at the fine print about how books under a certain dollar amount will be marked "Free" during the sales event.

Draft2Digital doesn't distribute to Google Play Books, so I have to upload my books there, too. So far, after a year, I have only sold two copies through Google, so I'm not sure it's worth the effort.

No matter where you choose to sell your books, there'll be the issue of pricing. Amazon offers two tiers for e-books, one with a 35 percent royalty and one with a 70 percent royalty. I don't know why anyone would choose the 35 percent option. With the 70 percent, you have to price your book between $2.99 and $9.99 USD. Look at what similar size books are selling for in your genre and set your price. The on-site calculator will then tell you how much you'll earn per sale.

The other sites I use aren't so strict. On Draft2Digital, you choose your price and the site will show you how much you'll earn for each retailer and per library checkout. On Google, you simply set your price.

Keep in mind that you need to be consistent across sites. You can't sell the book for $5.99 on D2D and $7.99 on Amazon. If you try that, Amazon will price match and lower your price there to be the same as other retailers, anyway, so just don't play favorites with the retailers.

If you want to play favorites, you need to set up your own store, which I've done. There are many options for this. I started with Gumroad, but wasn't happy with how the store looked, so, on the advice of

Joanna Penn, I switched to Payhip ... at about the time Joanna moved to Shopify. She, however, sells enough books to justify the upfront expense associated with a Shopify store. I do not, and Payhip simply takes a cut of each sale as payment for using their platform.

You can upload your books directly to Payhip for the customer to download, but if you do it that way, your books aren't watermarked and are easier to copy and pirate. So, when a customer buys from my Payhip store, all they get is a PDF card telling them to look for an e-mail from Bookfunnel. Bookfunnel.com will then send the customer an e-mail with a link to download their book. The book will be water-marked (if you selected that option in setup) and Bookfunnel will handle all the technical questions the customer might have. Payhip isn't so good about that and, from what I hear, you, the author, could be getting e-mail from your customers asking how to make the ePub file they downloaded work on their iPad or Kindle Paperwhite, or whatever. Do you have the expertise and time for that? I don't.

Amazon won't pay any attention to your personal store. At my Pahip store, I have all my books listed at 15 percent less than at the retailers I can't control. And I always provide a coupon code in my e-mail list letting subscribers get an even bigger discount if they buy direct from me.

Print books are different. There's a production cost, so Amazon, D2D, Ingram Spark (which D2D uses for print), and any other print publisher is going to set a minimum price based on the cost of pro-ducing a copy of your book. Then you get to set your profit margins.

There are some things to keep in mind when you are setting up your books through any of the big retailers. You need sales copy that will get the readers' attention. If you're like me and most of the authors I know, the idea of reducing your beloved baby that you spent months or years gestating, birthing, potty training, and whatever to a few paragraphs meant to make a reader open his or her wallet sounds worse than having your fingernails pulled out. I'll be honest with you, I have turned to artificial intelligence for this task. There's a site called Kinderprenuer.com with a feature that does exactly this. You type in your description and it reshapes and edits it into something that'll make your book sound like the next blockbuster.

You'll also need to research keywords for your book. This still seems odd to me. I don't go to Amazon and put keywords in the search bar. I look for authors or titles, but apparently some people will search for something like, "Books about coming of age with dragons." Will your book about a boy raised by a friendly dragon show up in that? Not unless you've used the right keywords. There are websites to help you with keywords. You'll need about eight of them, and they don't have to be individual words; they can be short phrases.

I'd love to tell you that my sales suddenly skyrocketed once I went wide, that Barnes and Noble customers were ecstatic to have access to my books and couldn't throw their money at me fast enough. But you know better. (This book's title, remember?) Some months my Draft2Digital sales are higher than Amazon's, some months Amazon is higher. I don't think I lost much in giving up the Kindle Unlimited perks, and I feel like my books are available to a whole lot more readers who don't want to use the giant Amazon.

Ultimately, which way you go is a decision you'll have to make for yourself. The good thing is, you're not locked in. If you go wide and don't like it, just remove your books and enroll in Amazon's KU and use the countdown and free book features you get as a KU author. If you try Amazon first and you don't get rich, end the KU agreement and try going wide.

Being an indie author is all about freedom. You get to decide almost everything.

Audiobooks

Once you become an independent author, you have to look for every way possible to sell your product. Audiobooks is currently the fastest growing trend in reading and publishing. I've been an audiobook reader for a long time and hardly ever listen to music in my car these days, choosing to listen to a book instead.

For a long time, the only game in town was ACX, which publishes to Audible.com, which is owned by ... You guessed it, Amazon.com. If you published your audio version through ACX, you signed an exclusive contract saying you would not make the audiobook available anywhere else. Audible.com dominated the market, so it wasn't that big of a deal to go with ACX.

Times, they are a-changin'!

But let's stick with ACX for the moment. The way it works is, you claim your book from Amazon, verifying that you are the author. Then you have to answer some questions, upload a sample of the book, and submit it. From there, you have a couple of options. You can sit and wait and hope one of the hundreds of narrators signed up on ACX will contact you with an audition, then decide if you like it well enough to pursue it. Or, you can browse narrators, using some pretty handy features that include gender, accent, location, genre, etc. You can listen to the narrator's sample and, if you like it, send them a request to audition for your book.

Some narrators will work for half your profit. ACX will split your earned royalties between you and the narrator. The good part is, you don't have to deal with making monthly payments to the narrator. The bad part is that the narrator gets half the profit for the life of the audio publication.

Other narrators want to be paid either a set price for the project, or per finished hour. Typically, you'll get better narrators going this route, so if you can afford it, this is the way to go, though I've had some pretty amazing narrators who worked for the royalty share.

Back in the chapter about technology, I touched on the boom in artificial intelligence. This is a major topic of discussion right now with audiobooks. Amazon/ACX/Audible has a beta program in which they are allowing computer narrated books. I wasn't invited to participate, so I can't tell you much about it.

Draft2Digital works with Findaway Voices for audiobook production. Findaway Voices is a rather complicated site to use and most of the narrators there do expect to be paid per hour of the finished product. However, D2D/Findaway Voices will allow AI-generated audiobooks. But to make that, you have to use another site, and there are many out there that will create an AI-generated audiobook from your text file, usually at a fairly high price.

This is why it's worth the effort to have your books in Google Play Books. Google offers this service for free. The voice options aren't as varied as you'll get with one of the paid sites, but you still get a pretty good selection. If the AI bot mispronounces a word, such as your weird author name, you can correct it.

To date, I've only done one AI audiobook, and it's my only book distributed through Findaway Voices, which distributes content to Spotify, by the way. I'm happy with the audio, but it isn't selling as well as my human-narrated audiobooks available from ACX. Your mileage may vary.

No matter how you do it, it is definitely worth your time to get your books out there in audio. I've had several months were my audio sales were higher than all my print sales.

Careful Spending

The thing with being an independent author is that you have to do everything. Every little thing.

Unless you hire it out.

Or have really talented friends who'll work for free or for dinner or beer or whatever.

I've created most of my book covers myself, and it shows. I'm not a graphic designer. Until recently, I fought the idea of paying someone to make a book cover for me, especially since my son told me he only enrolled in that graphic design course because there were cute girls in it, then his expensive Apple computer's battery swelled up and he couldn't do the work, anyway.

Nowadays, it's a mix. For my The Travels of Jacob Wolf western series, I'm still making my own covers in Canva. These are novella-sized books that are supposed to have a pulpy 1950s feel to them. Yeah, I'd love to have graphic illustrations of saloon shootouts on the cover, but you're talking serious money for that kind of custom work and, frankly, I don't have it.

For a couple of my bigger 2023 releases, I used Getcovers.com to create covers for *The Saga of Tarod the Nine-Fingered, Volume One* and *The Lost Pages Bookstore*. I love these covers, especially the fantasy novel, and they don't cost a lot. You can order e-book, paperback, hardcover, and audiobook covers, and there are options for various promotional supplies.

There are many sites online that will create covers or that provide pre-made covers the artist is selling and will take out the dummy text and replace it with your name and title.

GetCovers.com designed a very affordable cover for The Saga of Tarod the Nine-Fingered, Volume 1.

Unless you have some skill at graphic design, it's really best to have a professional make your cover for you. Even in an online store, the cover is your book's first impression with the reader. As I said about *After Obsession* in the previous chapter, the job of the cover is to get the reader to open the book, so it doesn't have to be an exact scene from the book. The little store on the cover of *The Lost Pages Bookstore* has very little resemblance to the shop described in the text.

Another GetCovers.com creation for The Lost Pages Bookstore.

Another thing you need to pay for is editing. No matter how many times you read your own work, you're going to miss something. You know what it's supposed to say, and so you skip over "there" when it should be "their" or "teh" when it's supposed to be "the" and, well, sometimes parts of your plot don't work or your blonde seductress leaves a raven black hair on the hero's pillow because you forgot that the day you introduced her you were having Marilyn Monroe fantasies, but then you saw the new Salma Hayek movie and wrote the next scene with the woman as a brunette.

There are many places to find an editor. Reedsy.com is probably your best bet. Fiverr.com is another option, but the people there aren't vetted like they are at Reedsy. Ask for references.

You need to know if you want a content edit or a copy edit. A content editor will look for plot holes and inconsistencies in your storytelling. A copy editor is looking for typos, grammar issues, and other mechanical flaws. Neither are cheap if they're good at what they do.

If you're lucky enough to be in a writer's group with actual professionals, you may be able to forgo this ... if you are good enough to provide the same service to your critique partners. Being an English teacher, I have friends who are also English and literature teachers who are my advance guard when it comes to editing.

After everything, your editing, your writing partner's editing, paid editing, and prayers and sacrifices, you'll publish your book and randomly flip through the fresh pages of your first copies and find a glaring typo. Guess what. You're an indie author and can fix it immediately. Nobody ran off 500,000 copies of your book with a typo and sent them to retailers all over the country.

So, you have your published book with a gorgeous cover and expensive editing. You've researched and used the best keywords, have great sales copy, and you've priced all versions of your book in a competitive manner. And it just ain't selling. What's a poor, frustrated author to do?

You're not just the author. Don't ever forget that. So far, you've been the author, the art supervisor, the editor-in-chief, and the publisher. Now you have to be the marketer, too. For many of us, this is the absolute worst part. Writing a 100,000-word novel is easy. Making people want to buy it? Please drag me behind a truck down a gravel road at high speed instead.

Your friends do not want a barrage of social media posts begging them to buy your book. Absolutely, you want to post about the book, and more than once. But your friends aren't your friends because they want to give you money, and even if they buy the book, they don't want to keep seeing you post about it. There are more subtle ways of doing this, such as posting pictures of a research trip you took for the writing of your book, or quotes from other works you read as research. But don't just crow at people about your book. You'll lose friends, or at least get muted.

Other authors don't want to buy your book, either, so don't try hawking it on your club's message board. Announce it and provide a link, of course, but only do that once unless some asks for members to post about their new releases.

You can set up a social media account specifically for book promotion. TikTok is especially good for this. Set up an account like Your

Name-Author and make cool videos about your book. This is not a strong suite of mine. My high school students have told me my TikTok content sucks. Compared to someone who knows that they're doing, yeah, it does.

Here's another little side note story. Be careful in making up your own hashtags. Pets are really popular on all social media. I had this idea of using my dog Bear as my therapist and recording videos giving him a human voice, offering advice and snarky comments about my attempt to make a living as an author. I called him my Bearapist instead of therapist. Cute as all getout, right? #bearapist The problem is that if all you see is the hashtag, it could be read as Be a Rapist. That's not nearly as cute. Be careful!

Also, cats are more popular than dogs on social media. I don't get it. Dogs are way cooler, but it is what it is. My cat Cleo is not a fan of me pointing a camera at her, but anytime I make a video with her, the views are way higher than anything else I post.

Where was I? Oh yeah, the hell that is marketing. At some point, you have to decide if you have the money to run ads. Amazon and Facebook are the most popular places for these as of this writing. There are books and YouTube video tutorials telling you how to do this. So far, I have only used Amazon ads.

The basic Amazon ad is easy to make because Amazon makes it using information from your book's sales page. All you really have to do is set your daily budget, and they'll even suggest that for you. You pay per click on your ad. I've never set a daily budget higher than $10, and I've never hit my budget limit. Read into that what you will.

My results with Amazon ads have been ... less than positive. My ad for *Shara* did result in a healthy number of clicks and some sales, but I spent more on ads than I ever made in sales for a month. My other ads performed even less well.

If you're running pay-per-click advertising, keep an eye on your ads dashboard so that you're not shocked at your monthly expense when Amazon withdraws their money from your bank account. If you're hitting your budget limit every day and you weren't prepared for spending $10 a day for 30 days, you can adjust your budget or cancel the ad at any time.

You can set up signing events at your local bookstores, but be warned that they will probably expect you to provide the books and then take a cut of your profit for providing the space.

Find conventions for your genre. If you can afford it, become a vendor. If you can't afford that, ask if you can be a panel participant so you get in for free. Prop up a copy of your book in front of you on every panel you're on. Carry a bag with a few copies you can sell if anyone asks. Encourage them to write a review of the book.

Always encourage anyone who buys a book to write a review! The more reviews you have, the more likely Amazon is to recommend your book to customers browsing other titles in your genre. Reviews are vital!

Some places that aren't book stores will take books on commission. Did you write a romance about a woman who runs a flower shop? See if local florists will put a few copies of your book by the register.

Be creative with your marketing. Don't do anything illegal, but otherwise, the world is wide open. Find ways and places where your book would appeal to people, and go for it. You'll be told no an awful lot, but not always.

Your best marketing tool for the book you've just finished is always going to be your next book, so don't spend all your time crafting the perfect ad or looking for just the right niche retailer. Write the next book.

Look at Me!

In 2016, when I was still teaching, the state of Oklahoma made yet another cut to the education budget, and there were bills in both the state House of Representatives and the Senate to make more cuts. The school I was at cut out a lot of extracurricular expenses, which had an effect on what I was able to do as the student council sponsor.

So, one evening as I was waiting for my wife to come home from work so we could drive to Tulsa to see Iron Maiden on their *Book of Souls* tour, I ripped off a blog post about how the cuts were affecting me and my school and students. No big deal. My blog typically doesn't get more than a handful of views each day.

At the concert, my phone kept buzzing with notifications. A few hundred people read my post that night. The next day, it climbed over a thousand. And it just kept growing. The local media outlets all interviewed me. Newspapers all over the country and as far away as England and Australia were writing articles and reprinting my blog. (*The London Times* used some godawful photos cribbed from my Facebook and I'll never forgive them for that!) *Good Morning America* called about having me on the show (we couldn't work out a schedule for that). Actor Ashton Kutcher tweeted out my blog. I went viral in a big way.

That post, just on my website, went way over 100,000 views with thousands of comments. That doesn't count all the places where it was cut and pasted and republished.

Kids at school were waving their cell phones at me while watching me on TV.

I just knew all this traffic to my website was going to result in book sales. How could it not? How could all these people not want to know more about the author of the blog post they loved so much?

Yeah, I sold maybe a dozen more books than usual over the next few months.

Being an independent author means you have the freedom to write what you want, when you want. But it doesn't mean anyone is going to care. To be successful, you typically have to offer a series with a lot of books. You have to work with the tropes readers want, and be ready to switch tropes when the population's tastes change. You have to take advantage of every opportunity to pitch your book to a potential reader.

Rejections won't come from agents and publishers. Rejection will come from friends who don't buy your books, from readers who ignore your new release announcement and your paid advertising.

Being an independent author is hard work. It isn't for everybody. Your chances of becoming rich and famous are probably at about the same level as winning the Powerball. Your chances of simply earning a steady living are only slightly better.

But you get to create, and you get the satisfaction of seeing your name in print, of holding a book containing a story you conceived and wrote, and that's something only a small percentage of people ever get to do. You get to leave behind a legacy.

Hopefully, you make a little money before you become yet another dead author.

A Case Study

This will not be an easy chapter to write. I have never discussed this issue in print. In fact, I have very carefully avoided it. Some detractors who may see this in the future will undoubtedly think this is simply me defending myself or trying to manipulate the narrative about this particular novel I'm going to talk about.

I include this chapter here is a cautionary tale to other authors of fiction. Think well and hard before you write anything even remotely resembling your personal reality, especially if you rely on that reality for your primary income.

The Background

What I'm about to relate as background leading up to the writing of my novel *The Teacher* is the truth, but it is the truth from my perspective. Other people may well see it differently.

At the age of 19, I married the girl I had been dating for almost five years. As time passed, we grew up and changed, developing different interests and beliefs and needs. In the summer of 2012, we came to a crossroads when my wife allowed our 17-year-old daughter to do something I absolutely did not support. Eventually, I laid down an ultimatum and got my way, but the damage was done. From that point, I felt like I was nothing but a source of income to my family. I was the bad guy they only tolerated for my paycheck.

I began having thoughts of driving my car off a bridge. Auto insurance would pay off the car, and I was carrying enough life insurance to pay off the house and all the rest of our debts. I could fulfill the only role I was expected to do, and wouldn't have to be the bad guy who insisted on rules and who, honestly, felt unloved at home.

Work was another issue. I poured all the love nobody at home seemed to want into my job and my high school students. I arrived early. I stayed late. I went to school events. I had drawers full of free snacks. I listened to students' problems and offered advice and got them help when I could. I wasn't an easy teacher. I made kids work, and they hated some of my work, but most saw later that I was really preparing them for college or jobs.

I co-sponsored two graduating classes, 2011 and 2014, with a female co-worker who, for many years, was my best friend. I was very close to the officers of both classes, but especially 2014. Beginning with the 2013-2014 school year, I also became the student council sponsor. My class and STUCO officers had my cell phone number and I had theirs. In fact, many students had my number. At the time, at that school, nobody batted an eye over that fact. Conversations were not inappropriate.

One of those students sent me a message saying, "Happy Thanksgiving!" at a big family gathering for that holiday. My mom told me I was too close to my students and that someday a teenage girl was going to get mad at me and cause me problems.

That started the gears in my head turning. "What's the worst they could do?" I wondered.

That question was the impetus for the novel.

The cover for my controversial novel, The Teacher.

The Novel

Even novels as fantastical as *The Lord of the Rings* draw upon real life experiences of the author. One of the most common pieces of advice given to young writers is, "Write what you know." So, it should be a surprise to no one that Andrew Clausing, the main character of *The Teacher*, shares many similarities with me, the author who was a teacher.

He is the student council sponsor at the start of the story. The opening chapter has him complaining about the use of glitter on a poster being made in his classroom, something I was well known for. All of the books he teaches throughout the story are books that I taught at some point, and all the lessons and insights are things I really shared with my students.

But there are notable differences. Mr. Clausing is younger than I was when I wrote the book. He's divorced, and I was still married. I have four children, but he has only one. He's very near to being classified as an alcoholic, and I very seldom drink alcohol.

Andrew Clausing is not me. In creating him, I used facets of my personality, altering or amplifying them as needed to create the character necessary for the story I wanted to tell. His name is a combination of St. Andrew, known for his strength and curiosity, and the Mr. Clausing who was my American literature teacher when I was in high school ... a great teacher with a flaw. The real Mr. Clausing had a quick temper. Andrew Clausing did not share that particular flaw, but he was definitely a flawed human.

Andrew is having an affair with his co-sponsor, a woman in her second marriage and the mother of two children. Her husband is a state congressman for the district where their school is located. Stealing a page from Nathaniel Hawthorne's "Young Goodman Brown," I named her Hope because that's what she symbolized to Andrew. Her last name is Daniels, again borrowing from my own high school days.

As the story goes on, an 18-year-old senior girl named Kelly becomes infatuated with Andrew. She drops hints, but Andrew is too naive to pick up on them. She begins to say things to other students and manipulates social media posts to make it seem like she and Andrew are in a secret relationship. At one point, she hides her cell phone in Hope's classroom to record video to find out what Andrew and Hope do in there during lunch.

Meanwhile, the head football coach is caught having an affair with a student. There's a scandal. Then the police break into his home to find him in bed with the student. The coach, surprised at the invasion, reaches for a gun and is killed. The message of this scene? The wages of this particular sin are death.

Along the way, we see Andrew interacting with his ex-wife and their teenage daughter. Both show obvious disdain for Andrew and only stay in touch to make sure the child support payments are coming and to demand money for other expenses. At one point, Andrew takes his daughter to an amusement park only to find that she'd arranged for some friends to be there. She ditches her dad, leaving him alone in the park.

Andrew, being an idiot, responds to a call for help from Kelly. She's at a party and wants to leave, but nobody will take her home. He goes and picks her up and takes her home. Other students record Kelly getting into Andrew's car.

School and district administrators call Andrew into the principal's office, where he is shown the video of Kelly getting into his car. He denies doing anything inappropriate with any student and tries desperately to explain the situation. He's shown other things Kelly has posted, and then the kicker ... the video of he and Hope making out in her classroom that was on Kelly's cell phone.

Andrew is fired on the spot. The possibility he's in an inappropriate relationship with a student is one thing. Messing with the wife of a congressman who could cut the school's funding is a whole other level of bad.

Andrew sinks into unemployment and alcoholism. His face is on the news. He won't answer Hope's phone calls for fear of causing her trouble. He's a teacher, so he doesn't have any savings. The rent on his apartment comes due and he faces eviction.

He does what, in his addled mind, is the only thing he can do. He goes to Kelly's house. She'd already texted him to say he could come and they would figure out what to do next. Kelly's guardian is her grandmother, a mean old drunk who is fine with her 18-year-old granddaughter being with a man in his forties. Late in the evening, she orders Andrew to go to the bedroom where Kelly is waiting for him.

In fiction, the hero must face the monster. He must look into the void and either conquer what he finds there, or die. Andrew enters Kelly's room to find her sitting on the bed in a negligee, surrounded by all the items of her girlhood. He knows she's no virgin, but the room is the room of a girl. She insists he sit on the bed, and he does so awkwardly. As she talks to him, he tries to make himself see the skinny student as a woman. Kelly reaches for him ... and Andrew runs out of the house. The next time we see him, he makes his second unsuccessful attempt at suicide. Because the wages of the sin he tried to contemplate are ... death.

He doesn't die. He tried drowning himself, but the rock he tied to his feet slips out of the rope and he surfaces, making the attempt a symbolic baptism and rebirth. Andrew sells or abandons all his belongings except what he buys for the new life he plans to lead, and sets out on the road, walking west with no destination other than some place where he isn't known to anyone.

The Backlash

I began writing *The Teacher* in 2015 and finished it in early 2016. I showed the first draft to a co-worker and to a senior female student. Both of them liked the story. The adult friend thought the two suicide attempts were hilarious. The girl found the first one horrifying and assumed it was something I'd actually tried. (I hadn't.) The adult thought the scene between Andrew and Kelly in her bedroom was too intense, but the girl who was Kelly's age was fine with it.

Here's another thing I share with Andrew: I can't read signals very well. This girl would later get the Othala rune featured so prominently as a symbol in my Werewolf Saga tattooed on herself in the same place the mark is put on newly trained lycanthropes in the books. She also sent me inappropriate photos once, then claimed she'd meant to send them to someone else when I asked why the hell she was sending those to me. I'm not including this just to be mean. This particular girl plays another role I'll get to in a minute.

Since this book is intended for authors, I'll go into some details non-authors won't care about. I wrote *The Teacher* in a new program

I'd just purchased called Scrivener. I loved working in Scrivener. I had notes on character sketches, the layout of my fictional school, and all kinds of stuff right where I could easily access them within the program. But, when it came time to export my book into an MS Word file so I could send it to publishers or agents, it was a nightmare. Every page was a text box, and they were not linked, and the margins were wrong. There were all kinds of problems that I could not fix. This was Scrivener 1.0. I'm writing this book in Scrivener 3, hoping that the problem is fixed because I really like the features. (Update: Scrivener 3 is better, but the transfer is still a problem, so I'm back to Atticus.)

The Teacher is written where every chapter begins with text messages, social media posts, blog entries, newspaper clippings, diary entries, etc., followed by standard narrative through Andrew's point of view. To make all this look as authentic as possible, I used different fonts, bold, and italics. What I finally had to do to have a manuscript I could submit was cut and paste every section, one by one, into Microsoft Word, then reformat it. I didn't want to do that. So, the book sat in limbo on my computer for a really long time while I worked on other projects.

It was late 2021 when I finally published the book. I posted about it on my Facebook, Twitter, my blog, etc. There wasn't a lot of fanfare, and even fewer sales. On Christmas, I texted "Merry Christmas" to my best friend. No answer. Same after my New Year's message. Then I saw a Facebook memory where she'd been tagged, but her name was no longer a link. Had she left Facebook? Nope. She'd blocked me.

Then I began to hear stories about students at the high school where I was teaching saying I'd written a book about a teacher having sex with kids. None of my students could tell me much more about it, and I honestly thought someone had gotten a copy of my horror novel *Mother*, which does contain graphic depictions of teenagers having sex with each other to make babies to feed to the monster, but that didn't happen until after they'd killed their teacher.

I was informed I would have to reapply for my job for the next year. Mind you, the assistant principal I reported to was supposedly a friend of mine from a previous school. I went through an interview process to keep my job, but I felt the vibe. On the last Monday of the school year, the little coward finally told me through e-mail that I would not be rehired. To this day, he has never told me why. I found out through a former mutual student that it was because of *The Teacher*.

I made a post on Facebook that nobody in their right mind had accused me of being a werewolf, but it seemed that some people were now labeling me as a danger to kids. And that's when all hell broke loose. One of my former class presidents, a young woman who had become a teacher at the school where I was just released, ripped into me for bad-mouthing her school. But that was nothing compared to my former student council president from the same year, who accused me of using real people in my book.

Then that former student council president went to her own Facebook and made two posts calling me a pedophile and a groomer. Because she is popular and influential, other former students jumped on the bandwagon. Kids who spent their lunches in my classroom voluntarily and came to me for advice and tampons and food were suddenly saying they never felt comfortable around me. I was horrified and, yes, heartbroken. They went so far as to contact the media and the state's secretary of education, demanding that my teaching license be revoked.

I got a physical proof of the book before release so I could go through and look at the complex formatting. There were a lot of errors that got marked and fixed. Then, I gave that marked-up copy to another former student because we were meeting regularly to talk about writing. Soon, a photographed excerpt from that copy showed up on the student council president's post because the writer girl was friends with that girl who got the Othala tattoo. Tattoo girl took a picture of the one paragraph in the whole book where Andrew tries to see Kelly as a full-grown woman, as if that was a fair representation of the whole book.

The next school year, I began at a new school on the other side of the OKC metro. The day before kids were to report, the principal came in and said we needed to talk about the message she had just received. Some woman I'd never heard of had sent a message to all the principals and superintendent of the school district, saying they'd hired a pedophile. Of course, no past employer had any complaint about any such thing. It turned out, this messenger had attended the same university as my former student council president during their undergraduate years. My principal had the curriculum adviser read my book, and she determined there was nothing inappropriate in it. Still, because I was "a risk for bad publicity," I was released at the end of the school year.

By that time, I'd gone to the teacher's union for legal help. The silence was deafening.

I retired from education to focus on my writing. I began running ads on Amazon and reading everything I could find on marketing and making a living as an author. But I couldn't do it. Without ever announcing it on social media, and leaving most of my friends to believe I was retired, I came out of retirement and got another teaching job.

The first day at the high school, the assistant superintendent of human resources pulled me from a meeting to say that sources at two of my previous employers had told him he shouldn't have hired me. I eventually learned they had told him about the book and the Facebook posts. They allowed me to finish the school year, then let me go.

The Lesson

Why have I included this horror story? I did it as a warning to you.

Did you notice I said nobody in their right mind had accused me of being a werewolf? That isn't the same as saying "Nobody ever accused me of being a werewolf." Because, there were such beliefs. Over the years, I've had several e-mails telling me I have to be a werewolf to write about them so realistically, and can I please make the sender a werewolf. No joke. But I never got called out on Facebook for being a werewolf. I never lost hundreds of friends because somebody called me a werewolf.

That former student council president not only called me a pe-dophile and a groomer, but accused me of putting real people in my book. She bragged that she had contacted every person I used in the book to tell them what I had done. The truth is that her graduating class was not as unique as she believed. The problems her peers faced — problems I assigned to students in the novel — were the same problems countless students before and since 2014 have dealt with.

She went on to make up an elaborate story about my writing process, how I had submitted the book to traditional publishers and they'd found the subject matter too disgusting to publish (I'm sure she's never read *Lolita*), and even went off about how I came up with the character names. She said the book is my "nonfiction sex fantasy where [I] get to have sex with students." She assured her audience that neither of the women Andrew Clausing has sex with in the book would ever really have sex with me. At one point, another former student tried to defend me, saying that the teacher killed himself at the end of the book and that all this bullying might make me do the same, and the response was that for what I'd done, I should kill myself.

Andrew Clausing never had sex with a student. He didn't kill himself. Neither one of those people read the ending of the book, apparently.

Andrew Clausing never had sex with a student. He faced that temptation, and fled from it.

And, oh yeah, he's a fictional character.

Hope Daniels also is a fictional character, but it seems that my former best friend felt that Hope too closely resembled her. It is true that some of the conversations between Andrew and Hope are very similar to actual conversations we had while working together, but I tried to make sure the character was different. The relationship was changed from friendship to lovers for dramatic effect and to provide another reason for the school to fire Andrew.

As a writer, you already know better than to use real people in your fiction. Even if you begin the story visualizing a real person in some role, you know that the character will grow and change and deviate from the model. But this is something people who don't write usually don't understand. "Am I in your book?" is a common question. Always say no. Always!

If you wrote about it, you must have done it, or at least thought about doing it. You're capable of doing it. That's another common belief about writers who explore dark themes. It's just as true as "Every romance author is a secret whore." In other words, it's not true. I know some authors who write sick, dark, violent, twisted stories beyond anything I could think up and they are some of the nicest people you could hope to meet.

Writers think about a lot of things we would never actually do. Does anybody really think Stephen King would dig up his dead son and rebury him in a pet cemetery so that he'd come back to life? Maybe. It's our job to imagine the fantastical, the horrible, the beautiful, and to craft it into a story that makes sense and restores a feeling of balance to the universe in the end.

The Teacher is a mix of my feelings about my family relations at the time I wrote it, built on a foundation of my mom saying I was too close to my students, and incorporating my experience as a real teacher. But just as flour and eggs and milk are not yet a cake, those pieces of reality become something else as you turn them into fiction.

Just be aware that there will be people out there who will accuse you of being what they think you've written about. I think *The Teacher* is a good story, but if I had it to do over again, I would either not write it until I knew my teaching career was over, or I'd publish it under a pseudonym and never let anyone know it was me.

To employ an old idiom, don't shit where you eat.

You've been warned.

CONCLUSION

Writing is a job. It's fun. It can be great therapy. You get to write the story you wish you could read. Other people might find your work and tell you that you're brilliant, or at least that you entertained them for a while.

But it's hard work. Sometimes the words won't come. When my marriage ended and I left my second teaching job, I entered an 18-month writer's block and deep depression and thought the writing might be over for good. Oh, I wrote a short memoir about teaching, a career I thought was over then, but that wasn't creative. I just couldn't find the motivation to write anything for a long time. Finally, I told myself I had to know if I was finished as a writer and pulled up the work-in-progress closest to completion and slowly — very, very slowly — got back into the groove and finished it. There were some 100-word days where I fought myself on every word. It helped that, with that book (*Sunset*, under my Adri Amanti pseudonym) I had a clear vision of the events that still needed to be written. Had it been a book like *First Born* where I sat down each day not knowing where the keyboard would take me, I couldn't have done it.

There's so much more to being a writer these days, particularly an independent "authorpreneur". Revising, editing, formatting, writing sales copy ... there are a lot of aspects to the profession that lack the pure joy of sitting at the keyboard and having a story spill from your brain as fast as your fingers can pound it out.

Then there's the marketing. Whether you're going the indie route, published with a small press, or got a big advance from a major house, it's up to you to market your book and get it in the hands of readers.

One book won't get you far. You have to produce more and more and be consistent to keep the attention of a fickle reading public. Failure to do that will result in publishers dropping you, or frustration and disappointment if you're doing it all yourself.

Days, weeks, months, years, and decades can slide by between your first publication and achieving your definition of success. And, honestly, you might never get there.

My definition of success is being able to make a living from my book sales. To be as transparent as possible, it is 2024 and I live in Oklahoma, a pretty cheap place to live. My regular day-job salary is about $54,000. I need to replace that amount with book sales to consider my writing career successful.

As of this moment, May 27, 2024, I have sold five books this month. If KDP and Draft2Digital were to pay out today, I'd get about $12 for the month. Most months, I can use my royalty payments to buy a decent dinner at, say, Chili's. Sometimes I can do something more expensive, like my favorite, Texas Roadhouse. Every once in a while I can afford to bring a dinner companion. That's my reality right now. With dozens of published books, I still have to rely on other employment to pay my bills.

One of the many groups I follow on Facebook is 20Booksto50k. The idea is that, once you have 20 books in print, you should be earning $50,000 per year. I'm at about 46 books and last year I made around $300 in royalties. Granted, the group has some stringent guidelines about writing in series, writing to market, only working in one genre per author name, etc. I haven't done that stuff for most of my career, but with my new Western series and new covers for The Werewolf Saga, I'm bringing some of my work in alignment with those ideals.

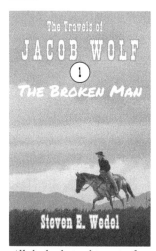

All the books in this series feature the same text layout and fonts with an easily identified piece of "Old West" artwork.

If you're reading this book, you probably already know a good deal about the real work that goes into trying to make a living or a name for yourself, or just finish a manuscript. It's work. But it's worth the blood, sweat, and tears you'll put into it.

Manifesting Habits

At the age of 58, I feel like I have spent my life waiting for my ship to come in, living the mantra of, "Things will be better when X happens." Often, X doesn't happen at all, or if it does, it comes with strings and complications I never foresaw.

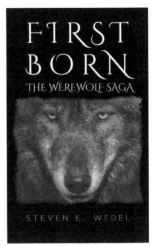

This has included my writing career. I'll make it when my first story is published. Nope. Okay, I'll get there when my first novel is published. Didn't happen. If I can just get a re-

All of The Werewolf Saga covers have been replaced with covers that adhere to the design of the most recent entry.

lease from a big New York City publisher, I'll take off and earn a living. Again, no. This next book in a new genre will put me over the top. A TV appearance. A viral blog post. A photo of myself with a famous author. None of those things worked.

I'm an optimist in the sense that I keep on believing that one day I will turn the corner and find fame and riches, or at least a comfortable income from doing what I love so much.

But ask anybody who knows me in person and they'll tell you I bitch and moan and whine all the time about jobs and the lack of success in my writing career.

I'm working on that.

I recently came across the concept of manifesting what you want. The idea is that you put out the vibe that what you want is coming to you and sooner or later, it will. It's a little more complicated than that, but that's the gist of it. Manifestation, prayer, spells ... it's all ritualized intent, as a dear friend of mine has pointed out. I'm trying to believe that I am a successful author so that I will become that.

I *am* a successful author!

You're sitting there, maybe sipping an expensive coffee or riding on your commute, smirking and asking, "Then why did you call this book *How to Fail as an Author?* That's not very positive." That's true, but we're not quite finished yet. No, I won't be pulling a big contract and bestseller status from my bag on the last page. The title of this book is meant to get the attention of its target audience and to be humorous, as I hope most of the chapters have been.

As I sit down to write each day, I repeat the mantra I have taped to the wall over my desk:

I will write books that people want to read.
I will write books that sell.
I will earn a living from book sales.
My books are good.

Is it working? Well, you bought this book, didn't you?

You Got This!

Even if you're working a full-time job in a factory or restaurant or anywhere else and writing in the spare moments at home when everybody else has finally gone to sleep for the night, you are an author. Whether or not you've experienced the first thrill of seeing your name in print, you are an author. Don't let anybody tell you differently.

I wrote five novels in the seven years I worked in a high production machine shop from 4 p.m. until midnight. I got up in the late morning, made a big lunch for my wife when she came home from her 8 a.m. to 5 p.m. job, then wrote for a while before going to my shift and again when I got home. That continued after the birth of our first child, with me often not getting to the computer until later in the wee morning and not until he napped in the early afternoon.

If you really want to do this, you'll find the time and the motivation.

Will you be successful? That's mostly up to you, but know this ... I believe in you.

I'm going to end with a quote that I feel makes the difference between a real author and someone who says they want to write a book. The quote is from celebrated author Octavia E. Butler. She said:

"You don't start out writing good stuff. You start out writing crap and thinking it's good stuff, and then gradually you get better at it. That's why I say one of the most valuable traits is persistence."

Persistence. Keep going. Your keyboard and your audience are waiting for you.

AFTERWORD

I hope you found this little book helpful, humorous, and inspiring. The road to success can be a long, hard trip, but with a positive attitude, persistence, and a little help and encouragement, we can get there. To that end, I've put together a workbook to help you along your way and you can get it for free since you were kind enough to purchase this book.

To get your free copy of *How Not to Fail as an Author*, please click on this link or copy this URL into your browser https://dl.bookfunnel.com/cnic29h8yb

You'll be taken to a landing page at BookFunnel, where you'll be asked to leave your e-mail address to be added to my newsletter, then you'll get your free 71-page workbook full of exercises to help you find the success you deserve.

If you prefer to have it in paperback, it's available at all the major online retailers. Of course, I can't offer the paperback for free because there's a cost to print it.

ALSO BY STEVEN E. WEDEL

Visit the MoonHowler Press store for these titles and more

www.moonhowlerpress.net

The Werewolf Saga

Shara

Ulrik

Nadia's Children

First Born

The Werewolf Saga: Apocrypha

Call to the Hunt

Murdered by Human Wolves

Cody Treat Series

Afterlife

The Saga of Tarod the Nine-Fingered

Volume 1

The Travels of Jacob Wolf

The Broken Man

Apache Justice

Warhorse Trail

Standalone Novels/Novellas

A Light Beyond

Amara's Prayer

Inheritance

Little Graveyard on the Prairie

Love Curse

Mother

Orphan

Seven Days in Benevolence

Shim and Shay's Wish

Songbird

The Prometheus Syndrome

The Teacher

Yes or No

The Lost Pages Bookstore

With Carrie Jones

After Obsession

In the Woods

Sleeper (coming soon)

Short Story Collections

Darkscapes (third edition coming soon)

The God of Discord and Other Weird Tales

The Zombie Whisperer and Other Weird Tales

Unholy Womb and Other Halloween Tales

Non-Fiction

How to Fail as an Author

Now Not to Fail as an Author (companion workbook)

You Want to Do What? Things I've Learned as a Teacher

As Editor

Tales of the Pack

ABOUT THE AUTHOR

Steven E. Wedel began craving fame and fortune in the literary world when he was in high school. After writing his way through careers as a machinist, journalist, corporate writer, and public relations specialist, he recently retired as an English teacher. He will keep writing despite the lack of wealth and notoriety.

Wedel has published nearly 50 books, mostly in the adult horror genre, but he's also written for the young adult, children's, Western, literary, and thriller markets. He's dabbled in other genres using pseudonyms. His non-fiction writing includes how-to articles for writers, literary criticism, and hundreds of articles for print newspapers, magazines, and online sites.

In 2004, Wedel earned a master's degree in liberal studies, creative writing emphasis, from the University of Oklahoma. He earned a bachelor's degree in journalism from the University of Central Oklahoma in 1999, and graduated from Enid High School in 1984. He is a lifelong Oklahoman, father of four, with four grandsons. He currently lives in central Oklahoma with his dogs Bear and Sweet Pea, and a cat named Cleo.

He'd still take the fame and fortune if it comes his way ...

Be sure to visit him online and sign up for his newsletter: www.stevenewedel.com